Main Men of the Seventies:

The Quarterbacks

By Jack Clary

A National Football League Book

A National Football League Book
Prepared by Creative Services Division,
National Football League Properties, Inc.
Publisher: David Boss
Editorial Director: John Wiebusch
Vice President-Operations: Jack Wrobbel
Managing Editor: Tom Bennett
Associate Editors: Tom Patty, Rick Smith
Editorial Staff: Patricia Cross, Earlene Doran
Designer: Amy Yutani
Production Manager: Patrick McKee
Production Staff: Rob Meneilly, Kathleen Oldenburg,
                    Jere Wright
Administrative Assistant: Muriel Lorenz

Library of Congress Catalog Card Number: 75-13796
Second Printing 1976
Printed in the United States of America

CONTENTS

A Quarterback's Work Is Never Done

All eyes seem to be on the quarterback in a football game.

Everyone in a stadium and millions watching on television know who they are . . . where they are . . . what they do . . . and sometimes what they can't do or didn't do. You probably know their names almost as well as those of your friends. Maybe you even see yourself being like them.

Perhaps that's why you sometimes stand before the bedroom mirror, watching yourself crouch before the dresser, barking out a cadence and taking that imaginary snap of the ball. It's why you bounce back a few steps, cock your arm, and let that imaginary ball fly and somehow hear the roar of the crowd as it salutes yet another touchdown pass.

Jim Plunkett did that when he was a kid. So did Roger Staubach . . . and Joe Ferguson . . . and Fran Tarkenton . . . and every other quarterback who ever has played in the NFL. And everyone who *didn't*, too.

It's very easy to do all the right things standing in front of a mirror. Oh, if only it were that easy on Sunday afternoons, say Plunkett and Staubach and Ferguson and Tarkenton . . . if only every pass brought the roar of the crowd. If only . . . if only . . .

You can hear them say it over and over during the week before a game because that's when they really work. There are no crowds roaring then, just the bark of a critical coach or the muffled encouragement of their teammates. There also are an almost endless series of meetings and miles of film that begin to flicker in the morning and don't stop until a player's eyes are red and sore late in the evening. There is the constant repetition on the practice field of running the plays that could be the difference on Sunday.

MONDAY: The next game begins. Some NFL teams no longer use this day to rest but bring in their players to check injuries, go through a brief workout, uncoiling sore muscles, and, most importantly, review the films of the previous day's game.

"It's a great way to forget what happened—good or bad—and start thinking ahead," Plunkett says as he hurries from his car on a chilly autumn morning and ducks inside the Patriots' dressing room at Schaefer Stadium. He joins his teammates and listens while coaches critique the overall team play.

At the Buffalo Bills practice site, Fer-

A quarterback needs to be a strong leader on the field; Fran Tarkenton takes charge in the huddle.

Following page: Anyone can pass in practice, but few can do it under pressure like Roger Staubach.

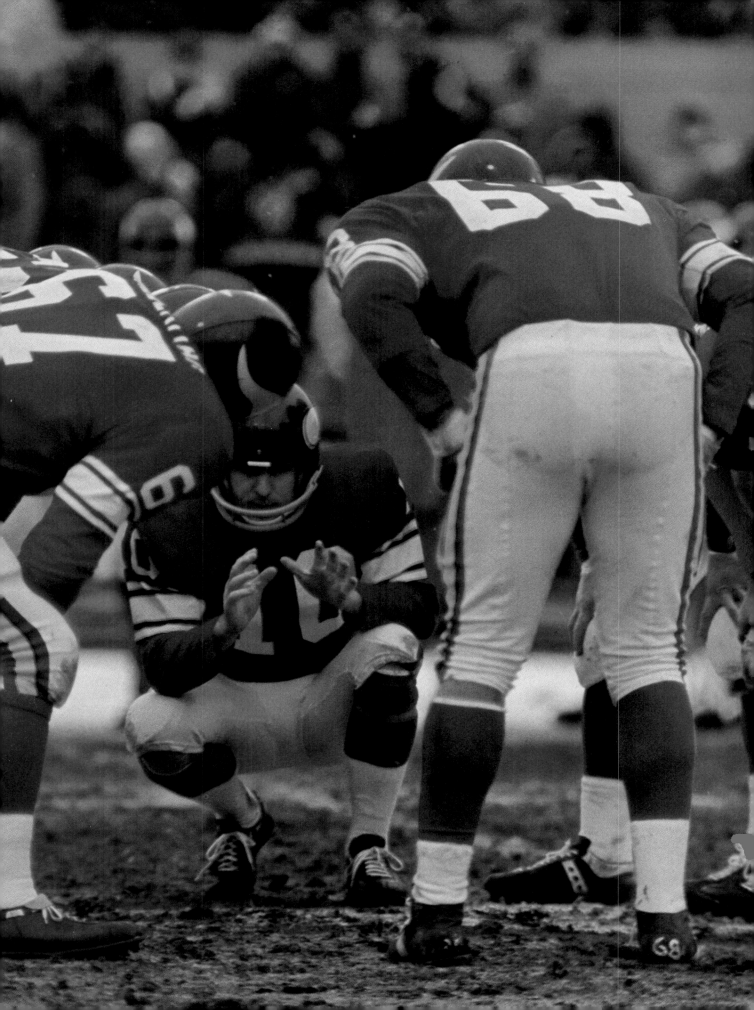

guson is doing the same thing and a couple of hours later Staubach sits with the Cowboys and really finds out what happened the day before.

All three quarterbacks meet later that morning with their offensive coaches and begin to lay out the plan for the next game.

There are few deep mysteries to making up a game plan. It is merely a list of plays that are designed to take advantage of an opponent's well-known weaknesses or tendencies. By itself, it is nothing more than an idea . . . a sheaf of papers containing diagrams that are given to each player. From it, will come victory or defeat.

Sitting with his offensive coaches, Plunkett hears what is planned for the next game. Does he have any other ideas? Are there any outstanding reasons why these plays won't work? Is it because of injuries? Or is it individuals beginning to break down? Or, perhaps, individual improvements?

"It's important for us to have Jim sit in on preliminary talks," says Patriots' offensive coordinator Red Miller. "We want to hear all sides, get all ideas and thoughts."

In Dallas, coach Tom Landry and his staff aren't as democratic on Monday. Their ideas won't be presented until the quarterbacks meet on Tuesday morning.

TUESDAY: A day of rest for most players on many teams. It is a chance for Plunkett to sleep late, allow his mind and body to finish unwinding from the last game. After a luncheon appearance, there are some afternoon errands and in late afternoon he sets up his movie projector. For the rest of that day, the reels of film unwind, clicking backwards and forwards as he begins to unravel the secrets of the next opponent's defense.

In Buffalo, Ferguson and the other Buffalo quarterbacks join coach Lou Saban. It is an afternoon at the movies here, too, as the Bills' staff discusses what they've planned. Ferguson is one of the youngest NFL quarterbacks and Saban takes as much care as possible to help him prepare. He points out the hesitation of, say, an out-

side linebacker in making his pass drops (play-action passes to his side should be effective) or the over-eagerness of a defensive tackle (the 32 trap with O.J. Simpson will go).

It's an hour later in Dallas when Staubach walks into Landry's conference room. Offensive coordinator Jim Myers joins them and they begin to outline the planned attack for Sunday. Roger offers a few comments and the coaches nod and offer their own ideas. A short time later, Staubach is alone in a room, watching more film. He takes the films home for a post-dinner movie session that lasts until nearly eleven o'clock that night.

WEDNESDAY: Perhaps the most important day of the week for a quarterback. This is "offense day." While the quarterbacks worked at home the previous night, the coaches put their finishing touch on the game plan. Now they must present it to the team and, in the opinion of Minnesota Vikings' coach Bud Grant, "convince the players that it will work."

That afternoon, the quarterbacks begin to perfect on the field what only has been on paper before this. Their defensive mates act as the opposition, using the same formations in order to give the offense a good idea what it will see on Sunday.

Each quarterback on the team runs five plays, giving way to the next, until every player involved in the game plan is thoroughly familiar with his assignment. If a play proves unworkable, changes are made on the spot. Questionable plays may be dropped altogether later.

This is a coordinated effort. Every coach makes suggestions, points out mistakes, offers hints, and, when necessary, gives some not-so-friendly criticism. Nothing can be left to chance.

That goes for after practice, too. The quarterbacks and coaches go back into another meeting.

"I'm not comfortable throwing the deep square-out against their weakside zone," Plunkett tells his coaches. "The cornerback keys the split end and he's too much in the pattern."

Sometimes the coaches agree. The play may be tossed out. Sometimes they don't

A quarterback must run at times, even if the play is unplanned (like Ken Anderson's touchdown run).

agree. Plunkett is advised to use some play-action, to "freeze" the back and thus allow the split end to get free sooner.

THURSDAY: The quarterbacks are in early again. The changes that were made by the coaches after they had left the previous day are explained. After another night of film watching, the quarterbacks offer even more suggestions.

In Dallas, Landry becomes a bit more flexible. Staubach tells him he's just not comfortable with a couple of plays, and they're discarded. In New England, the plan has tightened up and Plunkett must work to convince his coaches that changes must be made.

The meetings go on after the defense has worked against the opposition's offensive alignments. While this is happening, the quarterbacks often will be at the other end of the practice field working on pass plays with their wide receivers, sharpening their timing, making their own adjustments on the patterns.

"You work to establish silent communication," Plunkett says. "Your wide receiver lines up, sees the defensive backs in a certain position, and alters his pass route. He can't tell me when he's out there what he's going to do. But I see the same thing and I know what that man will do."

The quarterbacks leave practice late that afternoon and they've added some new films—a game against the same team a year ago. Another obtained in preparing for a game a month before. Before the week ends, they'll know what's on those films as well as they'll know their own offense. That's the idea.

FRIDAY: In Buffalo, Ferguson walks into Saban's office at 9 A.M. with the Bills' other quarterbacks. They'll spend an hour or so reviewing all that's been planned. By the time that meeting ends, it's now 9 A.M. in Dallas and Staubach joins other Cowboys' quarterbacks in Landry's office for a similar meeting.

This is general review day. The game plan is supposed to be polished enough to be completely familiar to every player and the drill runs smoothly.

In Dallas, the Cowboys are making changes. It is Landry's policy that his

game plan be 70 percent set by Friday's practice and the rest be put into sharp focus by the time that day has ended.

All the while, Staubach works on some of the more specialized elements of his offense—the goal-line offense that will be used inside the opposition's 5-yard line; the short-yardage offense for those vital third-and-ones, third-and-twos, and third-and-threes; the offense that will be used when a team is inside the opponent's 20-yard line, generally pass plays that must develop quickly because of the shortened area of the field, and, finally, the two-minute drill.

Plunkett's day is not finished. He's back at Schaefer Stadium at seven o'clock that evening for another round of meetings, films, and discussion. By nine o'clock, he and his coaches agree on every facet of the Patriots' offense.

SATURDAY: The work is done. The special teams get most of the attention during a short workout. By noon, the team either goes home or heads for the airport and a chartered flight to the opposing team's city. Rarely satisfied, the quarterbacks may spend an extra couple hours reviewing films that day, going over their check list of plays just to be sure.

SUNDAY: Through the week, the tension has built on the team as it prepared for this day. The whole purpose of a week's work is not only to run the right plays, but to be in the right frame of mind. No player feels this more intensely than the quarterback. He feels the same tensions as a defensive end or a running back, but, unlike other players, he cannot allow himself to become so emotional that he loses his cool.

All of the film study was to prepare him to recognize what the other's defense is doing. He must be able to apply what he sees in front of him with the correct play selection . . . and all in a moment of signal-calling over center. He must watch the actions of as many as eight pass defenders at one time, being careful within a span of just a few seconds to throw the ball where

A quarterback needs to be in touch with his receivers. So Tom Owen listens to Gene Washington.

it cannot be intercepted.

On the first series of play, he must begin to dominate the defense. Some quarterbacks feel they must attack the strength and if they can beat a team's strength, they can beat the team. Others prefer to jab right, jab left, probe the middle . . . all the while trying to find the soft spots. Once the weaknesses are exposed, the defense then must either cover them or live with them. The offense usually benefits either way.

At Schaefer Stadium this day, Plunkett has his offense moving smartly. It takes him just nine plays to get a touchdown, the score coming on a play-action pass to the tight end. Sure enough, the weak safety is held up just long enough for the receiver to get free.

In Buffalo, Ferguson has established O.J. Simpson's running, and the quarterback mixes his passing game smartly to keep the defense off balance. It was obvious the opposition was primed to stop Simpson and it takes its chances with Ferguson's throwing. So Joe goes to his passing game early. As soon as the defense begins to drop off and leave the line of scrimmage open, he sends Simpson swinging off the tackles. That's exactly what Saban had told him would happen while they spent those many hours together in meetings.

But things don't always go as planned, and often coaches and quarterbacks are forced to make changes during the course of a game. On this day, for instance, Staubach's running game is being stymied by the opposing middle linebacker, who gets into the flow of a running play as soon as it starts and succeeds in jamming it up.

The Cowboys had decided in the week before that their running game would be the key factor. So a change has to be made at halftime. In this instance, the coaches tell Staubach to make greater use of counterplays—plays that start in one direction but give the running back the option of cutting back to an open spot in the line.

At the same time, the linemen get better blocking angles on enemy defenders, who begin to cut back in pursuit.

Plays not working are discarded (some of them may be dropped even before the team reaches the halftime dressing room). The quarterback and the coach confer after every series. Plans are adjusted in areas where the opposition is successful.

In games such as these, quarterbacks must remain patient. A critical mistake such as an interception or poor play selection resulting in bad field position can mean defeat. And the more the standoff continues, the greater the tension . . . the greater the responsibility on the quarterback to deliver a victory.

Some quarterbacks—such as Staubach, Plunkett, and Fran Tarkenton—are agressive by nature. They won't take no for an answer. If there is no one open on a pass play, they'll run; if their running backs can't find room, they'll sprint away with the ball themselves, trying anything to create an improvised offense.

A game often will come down to which team has the last offensive series . . . how many times have you seen games won in the final two minutes because a quarterback has been able to move his team through a maze of defensive people . . . through the agonizing ticking of the clock . . . utilizing time outs and clock-stopping, out-of-bounds plays until somehow, someway, he gets the winning points.

On this day, Staubach did just that. He drove his team 97 yards in 90 seconds without a time out and there still were five seconds to play when the game-winning field goal sailed through the goal posts. He stood on the sidelines and heard the cheers crashing down.

This is the same man who stood in front of the bedroom mirror so many years ago. But this is the real thing.

It is another day in the life of an NFL quarterback . . . and tomorrow it will all be a memory, something from which to be learned. Tomorrow there is another team to prepare for . . . another game ahead . . . another week where there will be no cheers when the movie projector grinds or the coaches bark or the plays are run . . . and run . . . and run.

Terry Bradshaw listens to the advice of coach Chuck Noll during a brief moment away from the action.

KA

Ken Anderson   Cincinnati Bengals

Otto Graham had been an All-America running back in Northwestern University's single wing offense of the early 1940s. His only experience as a T-formation quarterback came while he played football in the Navy. So it surprised a lot of people when Paul Brown made Graham the quarterback of his football team, the Cleveland Browns, when they began play in the All-America Football Conference in 1946.

All Graham did at Cleveland was win— four AAFC titles, three National Football League titles in 10 seasons. Despite this outstanding record, Brown was criticized for sending the plays from the sidelines and Graham himself was belittled by those who felt a quarterback should call his own plays.

Now, more than a quarter of a century later Paul Brown is still at it with the Cincinnati Bengals. In 1971, he astounded many people by drafting a little-known quarterback named Ken Anderson from tiny Augustana College in Illinois on the third round. A lot of scouts thought Anderson had potential but few people expected him to be chosen as early as that.

Like Otto Graham, Anderson has given the critics some words to eat. He has become a successful NFL quarterback after just a few seasons and his future is unlimited. And, like Otto Graham, he still has his plays sent to him from the sidelines.

Because of this some have called Anderson "a robot." He's not disturbed by such talk. Those close to the Bengals marvel at Ken's even disposition. Some claim they never have seen him angry or upset; exhilarated or ecstatic.

He is not a robot, nor cold and emotionless. Rather, Anderson projects a great deal of warmth and enthusiasm about his job and about himself. He is a product of what some call "middle America," yet has a quiet sophistication that allows all who come his way to be heard and appreciated.

That includes Paul Brown. Anderson and Brown mirror each other's attitudes toward football, setting up an almost perfect rapport that has been largely responsible for Ken's quick ascent as an NFL quarterback.

It is hard to say which man has higher regard for the other.

"If there is any pressure playing in the NFL," Anderson says, "it is knowing that Paul Brown is a living legend. Heck, I used to watch the Browns on television when I was a kid. I knew all about them and Paul Brown. There was no way I could ever think that some day I'd be playing for the man. Yet here I am and now I see why his teams are so great."

Brown has unstinted praise for his young quarterback.

"He's like a surgeon," Brown says. "You give him enough time and he'll do surgery on your defense. He reminds me of what a great surgeon must be like as he wields a scalpel on an operating table.

"The reason? Because he is so disciplined. He works at being a disciplined quarterback. There just is no telling how great a quarterback he will become."

That appraisal is a far cry from the day Cincinnati drafted him. The first reaction was, "Who's he?" But the Bengals knew and so did every other NFL team because all had contacted him and had watched him during his four seasons at Augustana.

But Augustana is not Stanford, or Purdue, or Mississippi, and most pro coaches like their quarterbacks well schooled in big-time college competition. Brown appreciates the advantage of such football upbringing but he also looks at a player's character, his ability to learn, and his discipline.

"All of our people who watched him liked him," Brown says. "Still we wondered about making a kid from a tiny college a high draft choice. The day before the draft we looked at him again and could find no reason to change our minds."

The Bengals passed him on the first two rounds but when the third came, felt they'd pressed their luck far enough. It was a good thing because Atlanta was ready to pick him in the next round.

At that time, Cincinnati had Virgil Carter at quarterback. He had helped lead the team to its first division title the year before. They also had high hopes that Greg Cook, rookie of the year in 1969, would come back from a serious arm injury. If anything, Anderson was projected as good backup insurance.

In high school in Batavia, Illinois, Ken was an exceptional athlete and an excellent student. He went to Augustana to play basketball and baseball and it was only at the urging of his high school football

Ken Anderson runs a disciplined attack. Give him enough time and he'll take most defenses apart.

In his first season as a starter, Ken had the lowest percentage of interceptions in the NFL.

coach that he wrote and asked to try out for football.

"Sure," came the reply. "We need defensive backs."

Anderson answered that challenge but at 6 foot 2 inches and 210 pounds, he was as big as some of the team's offensive tackles. When the coaches saw him throw a football, they forgot about defense and soon he was the starting quarterback.

In the next four seasons, he broke every school record as a sprint-out passer. He also managed a 3.6 average on a 4.0 scale, majoring in mathematics. The talent for math has now helped him, say his pro coaches, in sorting out problems with defenses and coming up with the right answer.

But Anderson's biggest problem was winning a job with the Bengals.

"I was a bit worried when I came to camp as a rookie," he admits. "But after I saw the other pros, I really felt I could succeed. If I had any doubts at all, it was what would happen to me after that."

Fate helped. Cook failed in his comeback try in 1971 and Carter was injured, forcing Anderson into a starting job for five games.

"We had to force-feed him," Brown says. "But that put him way ahead of other quarterbacks who started the same season. His secret to such quick success is that he's smart and his poise was something unusual for a young guy."

That poise was quickly tested. The Bengals' fans, spoiled by the division title the previous season, became frustrated as the team faltered in 1971. They took out some of their frustrations on Anderson for typical rookie mistakes.

"I became immune to the boos," he remembers. "You must to succeed. I always was confident of myself and so were the Bengals. Everything came together with experience."

In the second season, he became the starting quarterback. Since then, Ken Anderson has come into sharper focus, as a player and as a person.

Otto Graham also had been called a "robot." But the difference between the two quarterbacks is that Graham did not like Brown's play-calling system and constantly fought with his coach to change.

"All that stuff doesn't bother me," Anderson says. "Actually, having the plays sent in takes off some of the pressure and frees me to concentrate on other things. Besides, I have the option to call audibles when I think they're necessary."

In Cincinnati's system, the plays are relayed from the coach's booth in the press box to Brown on the sidelines. He gives them to one of his messenger guards for delivery to the quarterback. But if the time comes, one of the Bengals' coaches says, when Anderson must call his own game, "there's no doubt in any of our minds that he could do it as well as any quarterback in the league."

He hasn't done badly under Brown's system. In 1972, his first season as a starter, he had the lowest percentage of interceptions in the NFL. Of the 301 passes he attempted, only seven were intercepted, a startling figure considering young quar-

terbacks find defenses so confusing.

The next season he became the third-ranked passer in the AFC and threw 18 touchdown passes as the Bengals won a playoff spot.

In a 1974 game against Pittsburgh, he completed 20 of 22 passes. The Steelers concentrated on stopping the Bengals' deep receivers, Issac Curtis and Chip Myers, so Anderson worked with his secondary receivers to upset the eventual Super Bowl champions.

"You see great quarterbacks do that," Brown says. "The rest will not look to see if there are other openings. That's where Ken's discipline and poise come to the fore."

That same season, he set an NFL record by completing 16 consecutive passes against Pittsburgh and Baltimore, over a two-game span. He didn't know there was such a record until after the second game.

"I looked at the play-by-play sheets later and my first incompletion in the Baltimore game that broke the string was on a deep post pattern to Issac Curtis," he says, laughing. "I guess the coaches upstairs didn't know about the record either or else they were going to make me keep it going the hard way."

He has no feeling for records. To him, they're fine after a career has ended and he might want to look back on his achievements. But it really doesn't mean much to him if he completes 20 of 25 passes and his team loses.

"If I complete five of twenty-five and we win, that's what counts," Anderson says.

That's been said before by many quarterbacks but somehow it has a lot more credibility coming from Ken Anderson because he practices what he preaches. The best indication is his effect on the team.

"When Ken first became a starter," Bengals assistant coach Bill Walsh notes, "he could run the team if it was going well. But he couldn't change things if they needed it.

"Now he can. He can pick up the team and carry it. He can score the touchdown from far out whether the team is going well or not."

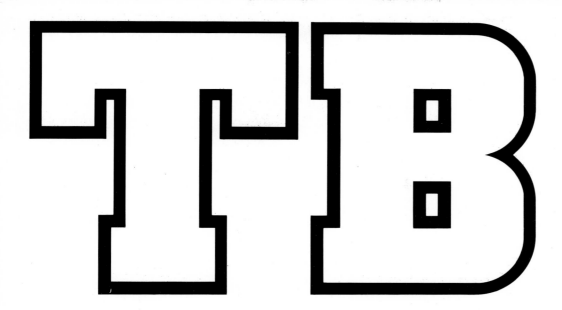

Terry Bradshaw   Pittsburgh Steelers

For most of the week prior to Super Bowl IX, sportswriters covering the game questioned Terry Bradshaw about his intelligence. Their questions really related to his ability to run the Pittsburgh Steelers' offense because he had gotten the reputation of being stupid. The writers not only questioned his thinking as a quarterback, but even his grades at Louisiana Tech.

Bradshaw answered every question patiently. No one likes to be thought of as stupid, and as the week went on, he volunteered information to try to break down such impressions. He pointed out that he received passing grades in college and that he received his degree in liberal arts, an achievement not every professional athlete can claim.

The Steelers, he added, would not be in the Super Bowl with a "dumb" quarterback, nor would they have made the NFL playoffs the previous two years with one.

Still, the doubts remained until the game itself, when Terry ran his team's offense almost flawlessly against the tough Minnesota Vikings defense. The result was that Pittsburgh won its first NFL title ever.

That is only one of the burdens the man from Shreveport, Louisiana, has carried since the Steelers made him the first selection of the NFL draft in 1970. In that time

he has been a living example that the greatest burden may be unlimited potential.

Almost everyone who saw Bradshaw play football in college and high school said his potential was unlimited. It still is. His throwing style is from a textbook—fluid motion of the arm as it sweeps past his ear, hair-trigger quick and with power, velocity, and range.

Though his blond hair is thinning now, he still resembles a comic strip character, Ozark Ike, whose muscles rippled with power; whose torso was hourglass shaped; and who projected a warm, homey, down-South manner. Some call it country-boy. But there is a great deal of right-now about Terry Bradshaw that projects itself every time he steps into the Steelers' offensive huddle.

That reality, warmth, and special sense of the super athlete shows forth in his daily life, whether in the operation of his Louisiana ranch or engaged in youth work, an area to which he devotes much of his spare time.

Terry always was a superb athlete, once hurling a javelin 255 feet in a high school track meet without practice. Some 50 college football coaches drooled over the prospect of him enrolling at their schools. Louisiana State University convinced him to sign a letter of intent but after visit-

ing much smaller Louisiana Tech, 75 miles from his home, he changed his mind.

It was then he first discovered pressure.

"When I signed to go to LSU," he recalls, "the girl I was going with back in Shreveport called me and said she never wanted to see me again. I live in Louisiana Tech country and I guess everyone expected me to go there.

"I did, but not for reasons like that. Tech ran a pro offense and used spread formations. I knew it would be the best situation for a boy who wanted nothing but to play pro football."

He was watched by pro scouts from the beginning of his college career. He could throw a football nearly 100 yards. At 6 foot 3 inches, 215 pounds, he was strong and had good speed. When he ran, he seemed to make it a point not to avoid tacklers but to try to bowl them over.

There was little doubt Bradshaw would be the top pick in the 1970 draft. The Steelers won a coin flip with the Chicago Bears for that choice and selected him. The Steelers knew they had made the right choice for at least two reasons.

First, Pittsburgh turned down 18 offers, each including a first-round pick, to surrender their place in the draft. One team is said to have offered four starters, a backup fullback, and a number one pick to have a chance to select Bradshaw.

Second, Terry's own enthusiasm was a bit unreal.

"I couldn't believe it when the Steelers called me," he says. "All along I wanted to go with a loser. I never wanted to go with Los Angeles or Minnesota or any good team. I wanted some place like Pittsburgh or Chicago where if I made it, they would make it, too."

On January 12, 1975, when Pittsburgh won Super Bowl IX, they "made it." But from the day he was drafted until that glorious moment almost five years later in New Orleans, it was not easy.

Pittsburgh coach Chuck Noll made Bradshaw the team's quarterback from

Coach Chuck Noll listens as Terry Bradshaw explains why he thinks a certain play will work.

the start, meaning he would have to learn through experience. He took quite a few lumps. As a rookie he threw six touchdown passes but had nearly four times that number intercepted.

"That season was a nightmare," he recalls. "I was bewildered, confused. Worse than that, I opened my big mouth too much and a lot of noise came back to haunt me. I talked a better game than I played and while some of the things I said probably were misunderstood, it would have been better if I hadn't said anything."

His inability to read defenses was the main problem, certainly not unique among young quarterbacks. Having only a fair running attack, Bradshaw's passing became the main thrust of the Steelers' offense for his first two seasons. As his interceptions increased, so did the dissatisfaction of the Pittsburgh fans. And the reputation of his being a "stupid" quarterback began to grow.

"I found out one thing in a hurry," Terry says. "There was a lot of difference between the NFL and the Gulf States Conference where Louisiana Tech played.

"I had to mature both on and off the field in those early seasons. I'm not sure I would change anything that happened. You have to find out what it's all about in pro football and, in my case, that meant growing up."

With all of that, it took another excellent draft by the Steelers to help Bradshaw. In 1972, Pittsburgh selected running back Franco Harris, then traded for John (Frenchy) Fuqua to join their best runner at that time, Preston Pearson.

"After relying on passing for my first two years, our running game began to carry the load," Bradshaw recalls. "That meant I passed less and in many situations where the defense didn't really know whether or not Franco was coming."

He had thrown 373 passes in 1971 but threw only 308 in 1972. He was intercepted 22 times, only 12 the next season. And the Steelers made it to the NFL playoffs for the first time since the team was founded 40 seasons before.

Few gave Pittsburgh much of a chance

against Oakland in the first playoff game and even owner Art Rooney had left his seat with two minutes to play after his team finally lost the lead. Many of the thousands who jammed Three Rivers Stadium in Pittsburgh also had left before Bradshaw faded to throw his final pass.

The ball was intended for Fuqua but Oakland defensive back Jack Tatum deflected it. Trailing the play, Franco Harris caught the ball inches off the turf and ran for the winning touchdown. It was one of the most electrifying plays in NFL history.

Pittsburgh lost to Miami in the AFC title game the following week but, at last, the Steelers had emerged as a contender. It wasn't all Bradshaw and Harris because Pittsburgh's defense had gained even greater recognition. But one without the other could not sustain the team's newly found success.

Terry also began the next course in his pro football schooling: The pass would be secondary to the run. Most NFL coaches, including Noll, had put greater emphasis on running because the zone defenses utilized linebackers and defensive backs to such a great degree. There was more room to run; less to be gained from passing.

"All my life, my play calling had been geared to the pass and I never really understood the running game," Bradshaw says. "But with guys like Franco, you have to run the ball. It's been a tough adjustment but one that I seemed to have worked out."

The biggest adjustment came in the 1974 season when he lost his starting job to Joe Gilliam. For the first six games he sat unhappily on the bench while the younger man started. But inexperience showed and the Steelers began to stumble.

Noll called on Bradshaw once more and Terry started all but one of the team's remaining games. His best efforts came in the AFC playoffs when the Steelers beat Buffalo and Oakland to reach the Super Bowl. In the Oakland game, he completed 9 of his 14 passes for 96 years and one touchdown, and ran five times for 33 yards.

"My dad had told Mr. Rooney when I signed five years before that in five years the Steelers would win the Super Bowl," Terry recalls. "I don't believe in stuff like that but look what happened."

Former quarterback great Y.A. Tittle once said, "Bradshaw has the best arm I've ever seen."
Right: Terry eludes Minnesota's Alan Page, one of the NFL's leading defensive tackles.

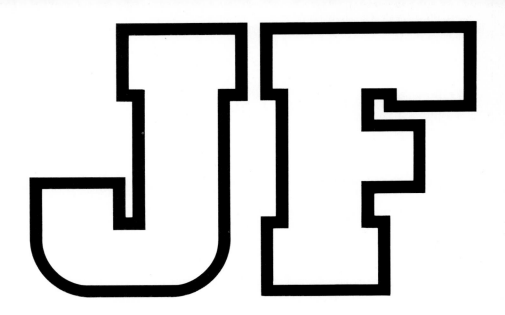

Joe Ferguson   Buffalo Bills

The clock on the scoreboard in Buffalo's Rich Stadium had stopped with two minutes to play.

OAKLAND 13, BUFFALO 7

BALL ON: OAKLAND 8

Millions of television viewers and 80,000 fans in the stadium watched with anticipation on the first Monday night of the 1974 season as Bills quarterback Joe Ferguson stood behind his center, ready to receive the ball. As it smacked into his hands, wide receiver Ahmad Rashad sped toward the end zone, faked to the outside, then broke past Oakland's Skip Thomas and slanted across the goal line.

As his feet touched the end zone, Ferguson's pass drilled into his hands. Touchdown! Extra point: Good.

BUFFALO 14, OAKLAND 13

TIME TO PLAY: 1:56

While those 80,000 fans let loose a deafening blast, not too many moved to leave because the dangerous Raiders—dangerous because they had George Blanda's right leg—still had a chance. But when three of Ken Stabler's passes fell incomplete and forced a punt with 86 seconds to play, the game was over.

Or was it?

There was no O. J. Simpson to fall back on. He'd injured his ankle late in the first half and could not play. Still, what could

happen in 86 seconds?

On the first play, Bills fullback Jim Braxton fumbled the ball trying to run outside. Oakland defensive tackle Art Thoms picked it up and raced for a touchdown.

OAKLAND 20, BUFFALO 14

TIME TO PLAY: 1:14

Fans recalled the previous season. When the team got behind and needed a quick score, miracles just don't happen. Buffalo had built its offense around "The Juice" and it was a ball control, grind-it-out game that consumed minutes, not seconds. Now there was no O. J.

Starting at his 28-yard line, Ferguson showed something not seen in his rookie season. He could pass, just as the scouts, his coaches in high school and college, and most of all himself knew he could. Pass-pass-pass, a couple of major penalties, and Buffalo was on Oakland's 12-yard line.

Hardly looking up, Ferguson brought his team out, sent Rashad against all-pro cornerback Willie Brown and rifled another pass into the end zone. Rashad turned Brown around and sped to make the catch.

Touchdown! Extra point by John Leypoldt.

BUFFALO 21, OAKLAND 20

TIME TO PLAY: 21 SECONDS

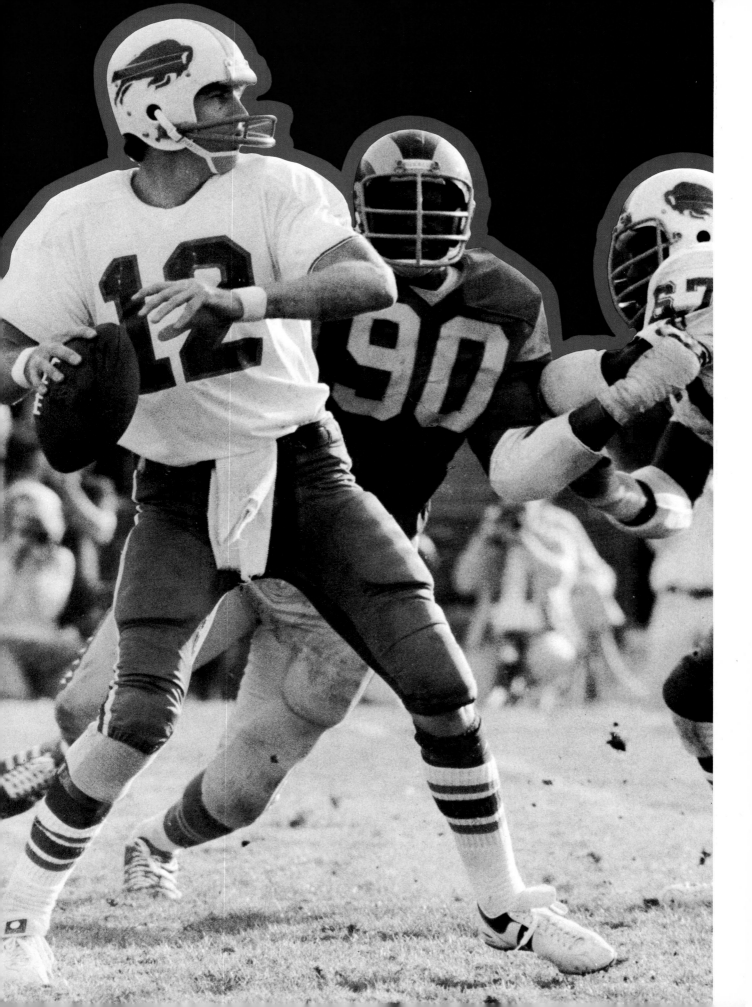

In 53 seconds, or twice within a minute and a half, Joe Ferguson showed what the new-look Buffalo Bills would become. When the 1974 season ended, the Bills made the playoffs for the first time since 1966.

Why?

One big reason is they had a real quarterback, one who could pass. No longer could defenses be stacked to stop O. J. It was something not many Buffalo opponents figured would happen . . . at least, not so soon.

As a rookie quarterback in 1973, Ferguson did little more than hand the ball to Simpson and stand back and watch him run for a record-setting 2,003 yards. He didn't call his own plays, he threw only 164 passes, and only four of his passes went for touchdowns. If anything, that season was a tribute to O. J.'s running and the blocking of the offensive line. Ferguson was almost a spectator.

That was part of coach Lou Saban's plan to develop his young quarterback. It was directed at building his confidence because everyone, from the coaches to the forty-seventh player, knew Ferguson

Joe is intense during a lull in the locker room before a game.
Left: Joe Ferguson looks downfield for his primary receiver as Los Angeles's Larry Brooks closes in.

could pass. He had proven that one day early in his first Bills training camp when he completed eight passes in a row against the team's number one secondary. That was the day he assured himself the number one quarterback's job.

Saban's system didn't make him totally unhappy. He would have liked to call his own game—what quarterback wouldn't?—but he saw the merit of his coach's way. If anything, he probably was happy out of the limelight.

"People weren't expecting a lot of me," he says, "so it gave me a chance to come along slowly and learn. I would throw in certain situations but mainly it was a learning process.

"In 1974, it became a lot more enjoyable to know that I was contributing instead of just giving off the ball and watching."

Ferguson made major contributions to Buffalo's playoff march. There was a game in New England against the Patriots with first place in the AFC East at stake. Ferguson completed seven of eight passes in the first half, got three touchdowns and the Bills led 27-14.

In the second half, he threw just four times and his only completion came on third-and-21—22 yards to Rashad that set up the decisive field goal by Leypoldt in a 30-28 victory.

Ferguson broke all of Terry Bradshaw's passing records at Woodlawn High School in Shreveport, Louisiana, and some people there claim he'll finish his pro career as a better passer than Bradshaw. He was one of the most sought high school quarterbacks in the South before deciding to enroll at Arkansas.

In some ways it was a difficult choice. After he had decided on Arkansas, Louisiana Governor John McKeithen paid a personal visit to his home to persuade him to attend LSU. How many high school kids get that kind of treatment?

"My mind was made up, though," he recalls. "Arkansas was one of the few colleges using a pro-style offense and I liked to throw the ball."

He did so well at Arkansas that after his junior year, he was touted as most likely

to win the Heisman trophy in 1972. Then his world turned upside down. He had difficulty adjusting to a new backfield coach, a new offensive system, and several new receivers. After the Razorbacks lost their first game to USC, it became a struggle.

Finally, coach Frank Broyles installed the wishbone T offense for the last two games and Ferguson watched from the bench. His potential as a pro quarterback was questioned by some, at times by Joe himself. That's why he says, "People weren't expecting a lot of me."

Broyles never had any doubts.

"We just didn't have enough to help him in his senior year," the coach admits. "Joe was the finest passer I've seen in college but we couldn't protect him and we didn't have enough runners to take the pressure off."

Every NFL team shied away during the first two rounds of the 1972 draft until the Bills, with the sixth pick of the third round, decided he was worth the risk. Saban was ready to demote holdover quarterback Dennis Shaw whose offensive style was in direct contrast to his coach's conservative philosophy.

Ferguson joined the Bills knowing how a pro offense should be run, how to read keys when attacking a defense, and with plenty of raw talent. Though he missed three weeks of training camp working with the College All-Stars, it didn't seem to matter.

He was Buffalo's quarterback when the Bills opened their new stadium in a preseason game against Washington. He threw three touchdown passes—something Buffalo fans would not see the rest of that season.

"My real break was having O. J.," Ferguson admits. "If he hadn't been around I don't know whether I could have made it as a rookie. If we would have had to come out throwing right away, it would have been awfully tough.

"I was able to look at defenses and learn. I didn't have to throw into them and get my brains beat out."

It was Saban's idea that Ferguson not only know when to throw the ball but why. Thus the reliance on Simpson. When

Joe prefers to throw from the pocket, but if he has to, he can throw while rolling to either side.

Joe did pass, it was what coaches call "high percentage"—a pass that was least likely to be intercepted.

That helped build a more conservative philosophy on the field because Ferguson is not a wild flinger. In his first two seasons, 22 of 396 passes were intercepted.

His own style helps. Ferguson is not big at 6 foot 1 inch and 180 pounds, but he is mobile. He's good with play action and he can throw well while rolling out to either side. He disdains the run if possible but is a clever, quick runner when the situation demands.

When he stands in the pocket, he's most dangerous. Buffalo's receivers say he's above average for his ability to drill the ball into tight places as he did in the Monday night game against Oakland in 1974. That's something he didn't do as a rookie.

In the first 10 games that year, he threw just one touchdown pass as Simpson roared toward the new rushing record. But, with Buffalo in a three-game losing streak, he offered a glimpse of what the real Ferguson could do against Baltimore.

The Colts led 17-10 with 94 seconds to play when Ferguson hit Bob Chandler with a 37-yard touchdown pass. Leypoldt's extra point tied the score and moments later defensive back Dwight Harrison intercepted a pass by Marty Domres and ran for the winning score. Without Ferguson's touchdown pass, Domres never would have had to pass.

That began a season-ending, four-game winning streak. But Ferguson had proven to Saban, his teammates, and himself that he could deliver the key pass in the NFL when it was needed.

"You could see the confidence grow after that game," Chandler recalls. "I think he always wondered whether or not we were behind him until that game. We were but he proved a lot to himself that day."

In 1974 he proved even more by guiding the Bills to the playoffs.

"The difference," O. J. Simpson says, "is that I was the main man in 1973. In 1974, we had more variety because everyone found that Joe Ferguson could play football. No defense ever could gang up on us again."

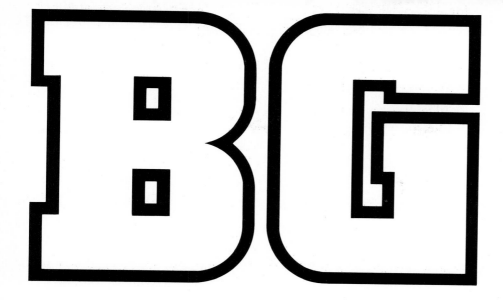

Bob Griese   Miami Dolphins

It had been a miserable week for Bob Griese. Weakened by a virus, he had dragged himself through five days of practice with the Miami Dolphins. No matter what kind of medication he tried, nothing seemed to work. On a balmy Miami Saturday evening, everything came apart.

"We had to rush Griese to the hospital," the team doctor told coach Don Shula by telephone that night. "He might be able to leave in the morning and he could be in uniform. But he'll be too weak to play."

The Dolphins were to play Pittsburgh the next day. Miami had won five games in a row and was in a two-team race with Baltimore for the American Football Conference's Eastern Division title. The Steelers were not supposed to be much of a problem but Shula was bothered by the thought of not having a healthy Griese.

There was nothing Shula could do but start backup quarterback George Mira and hope for the best. Near the middle of the second quarter, the Dolphins trailed 14-3 and their offense had all but stopped.

Shula turned to Griese, who was standing next to him on the sidelines.

"Ready?" he asked.

"Yeah," Bob replied. "I'll give it a shot."

On the first play, he fumbled and lost the ball. Pittsburgh converted that mistake into another touchdown and a 21-3

lead, with more than half the second quarter still to play.

But one of Bob Griese's major strengths is his ability to remain cool. Long before that November Sunday he had been a winner when the Dolphins were losers because he refused to hang his head or give up.

And so in the next seven minutes of the game against Pittsburgh, Bob threw a pair of touchdown passes to Paul Warfield and then got the winning touchdown in the fourth quarter.

It's not that Bob is unemotional, it's just that he takes things in stride. It's the way he operates every day—in practice, in a game, or even in the Super Bowl. The first time Miami played in the Super Bowl, in Game VI against Dallas, Griese tried to scramble out of trouble in the persons of Cowboys linemen Bob Lilly and George Andrie.

Back . . . back . . . back, he pedalled, desperately trying to escape the two huge linemen. But few ever dodged Bob Lilly in his prime and the Cowboys' tackle caught Griese and hurled him to the ground for a 29-yard loss.

After the game, Griese shrugged off the play.

"I've been tackled before trying to pass and I'll be tackled again," he said. "It was just one play that didn't work."

"It's funny," a friend says, "but when the Dolphins run onto the field with their aqua and orange and white colors, I expect to see Bob come trotting out wearing charcoal gray. It's just the way he is."

"The way he is" . . . well, he certainly does not epitomize the free-wheeling, high-spirited attitude of some of his teammates, or for that matter, of many of the other NFL quarterbacks. Instead, he is serious, single-minded, all-business, self-contained and, except among those who are close friends or teammates, seemingly without a sense of humor.

Some say Griese is out of the mold cut by Bart Starr when he helped guide Green Bay through its succession of championships playing for the late Vince Lombardi.

But no matter how Griese is characterized, one trait has run through his career from high school in Evansville, Indiana, to college at Purdue and with the Dolphins. He is a winner.

When the Dolphins won consecutive Super Bowls in 1973 and 1974, the most unsung of its many stars was Griese. Even usually anonymous offensive linemen got more publicity. All Griese did, many said, was hand the ball off and let Miami's punishing ground attack pulverize opponent after opponent.

It may have seemed that way, but it just wasn't so. While many NFL quarterbacks spend hours studying films of opponents' pass defenses, Griese spent just as much time studying the way the opposition would defend against a running game. Then he would direct his attack, knowing exactly where the weak spots would be.

And he'd be just as prepared to attack the pass defenses. Every time an opponent became overly conscious of his runners, he'd deliver a perfectly thrown pass to Paul Warfield or Howard Twilley, or another of the team's outstanding receivers. Like Bart Starr, he is a master of keeping the opposition off balance, not allowing it to know from where the next blow will come.

"Passing is about fifty percent of my job," Griese says. "I study as much on the running game as I do on the passing game. I talk to the offensive line coach as much as I do the receiver coach. A quarterback had better have an understanding of the passing game but he also must understand the running game. When to call it is the thing.

"And," he adds, "you don't make a living on the long pass. I always felt I had to be sound on my short and medium passes first and then take the long one when it came."

That thinking caused doubt about his ability to be a good passer in the NFL after the Dolphins selected him as the fourth pick on the first round of the 1967 draft. Overcoming those doubts and improving his skill was just another day's work for him. He'd been used to such things since early in his teens.

"My dad died in his sleep when I was twelve and his death had a big effect on me," he says. "I turned more toward sports but I also listened more attentively than most boys to what coaches told me because I didn't have a father at home to teach me. A father is really a coach and my coaches became substitute fathers."

He had hoped to attend Notre Dame but was rejected as a quarterback prospect because coaches felt he was too small at just a shade over six feet. He went to Purdue as a sidearm quarterback, but he played safety on defense as a freshman while coaches worked to improve his passing style.

"Bob just couldn't throw a good ball when he was a freshman," one of his Purdue coaches said. "He got rid of it quickly but it didn't spiral. He was trying to force his release, which meant he was throwing the ball with the nose down, sort of pushing it."

That flaw corrected, Griese became an excellent college passer and in his senior year he helped Purdue to victory in the Rose Bowl. Still, there was the question of his ability to throw long, though not in the minds of the Dolphins. To Miami's scouting department, he was the quarterback of their future. The Dolphins had decided to pick him over local favorite Steve Spurrier, who that season had won the Heisman trophy playing quarterback for the University of Florida. Spurrier seemed a natural selection for a team in

Bob has come a long way from his days as a freshman at Purdue, when he had trouble throwing a spiral.

just its second season and trying to attract customers, but there was little doubt in the minds of team officials that Griese would be a better quarterback over the long run.

Bob signed a four-year contract to play for the Dolphins. He gave some of the bonus money he received to his brother and sister to pay their way through Purdue. That was an early indication of his own unselfishness, a trait that has been recognized and appreciated by his Dolphins' teammates.

Another indication came a month before he was drafted by Miami. He almost lost his own life trying to rescue a friend from the surf in Hawaii while in Honolulu to play in the Hula Bowl.

Few rookie quarterbacks have begun their NFL careers more dramatically. The Dolphins opened the 1967 season with John Stofa as the starter but early in that first game, he broke his ankle. Griese took over. When he had finished, completing 12 of 19 passes, Miami had a 35-21 victory over Denver.

No one ever took the job from him again. In those days, the Dolphins were still building an expansion team and Bob didn't enjoy the good blocking he has today. He'd often retreat to pass and wind up running for his life, solidifying the reputation as a "scrambler" he had brought from Purdue.

It wasn't until Shula became Miami's head coach in 1970 that Griese began to mature. Shula believed a quarterback passed best from the pocket. The coach worked with Bob to remain in his pocket, helping him by improving the Dolphins' offensive line and giving his quarterback a much more varied offense.

In 1972, Bob broke his leg and was sidelined for the last nine games of the regular season. But he returned to drive Miami

through the playoffs, including a 14-7 victory over Washington in Super Bowl VII that climaxed the first perfect season for an NFL team since 1942.

The following season, he helped lead Miami to another Super Bowl victory, this time crushing Minnesota 24-7. He threw only seven passes but completed six while Miami's running game, led by Larry Csonka, pounded through Minnesota.

Griese is proud of his role in Miami's success. He makes no excuses for having an all-business approach to his job, nor for being classified as conservative, aloof, quiet, reserved.

"I'm more of an introvert than an extrovert," he admits, "but I don't think I'm a quiet person. I'm not boisterous or outspoken. But if there are a bunch of football players ready to play football, somebody has to be in command.

"Taking command, that's something that somehow I've always been able to do."

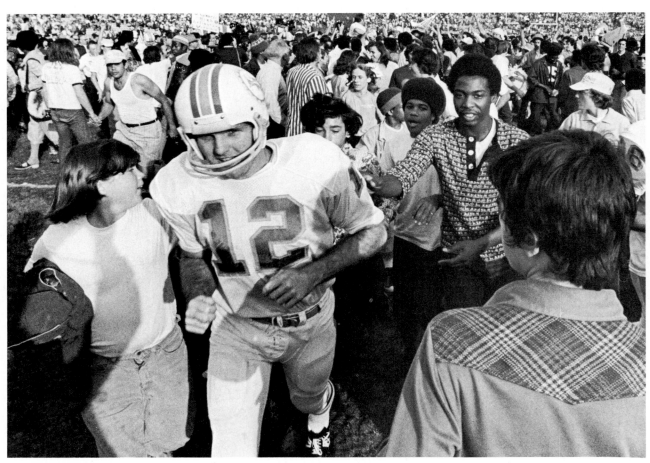

Bob Griese wears the look of victory that symbolized the Dolphins' 17-0 perfect season in 1972.
Right: Bob listens as coach Don Shula points out weaknesses in the opponent's defensive secondary.

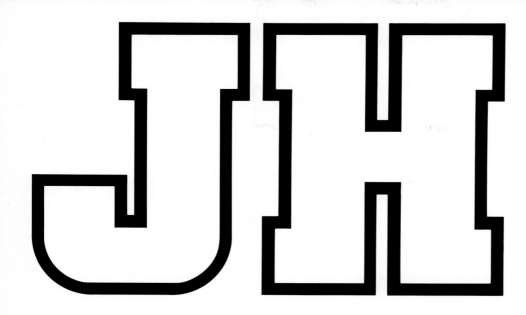

James Harris   Los Angeles Rams

The pro football world was stunned. John Hadl, who had guided the Los Angeles Rams to a division title the year before, had been traded to the Green Bay Packers. This was the same John Hadl who was chosen the NFC's most valuable player, the same quarterback who seemed to have the Rams heading for another title.

That was only part of the surprise. Los Angeles didn't trade for another top quarterback. The Rams said that their number two quarterback was good enough to do the job.

Hadl, and Roman Gabriel before him, had dominated the Rams' offense. Few people except for diehard Los Angeles fans, even knew Harris's name.

That was nothing new to James Harris. He knew what it was like to be forgotten, overlooked, and unseen. A lot of fans had forgotten that he existed, though five years before, in 1969, he was called a pioneer, a man who would break a barrier of sorts that had existed in the NFL throughout its modern era.

But this was 1974 and it took a bit of memory jogging to remember that James Harris was supposed to become the first black man ever to be a starting NFL quarterback—the first one with a solid chance to keep the job. He was no Jackie Robin-

son because the NFL long ago—even before Robinson was signed by the Brooklyn Dodgers in 1946—had broken that racial barrier.

Harris played college football at Grambling College, where Eddie Robinson was his coach. Robinson knew that a quarterback has to have intelligence, an outstanding throwing arm, and the size and stamina.

In Harris, he knew he had a man who met the qualifications. And when the 1974 season ended with the Rams in the NFC playoffs, Robinson's judgment was supported. It just took longer than he—or Harris—ever imagined.

James Harris proved to be a worthy pioneer but he did it by first making Los Angeles forget John Hadl. Helped by plays being called from the bench, Harris executed as though he were a 10-year veteran. He had poise, he had a much stronger arm than Hadl, and he was more mobile.

People seeing him for the first time were impressed by that poise. If possible, he'd stay in the passing pocket and throw, even with the likes of Carl Eller or Alan Page or Claude Humphrey ready to bury him. If chased out of the pocket he would seek out the open receiver, never seeming to be in a panic. When he did run, his 6-foot 4-inch, 210-pound frame punished tacklers.

He had complete confidence in his skills. There is not a receiver in the NFL, he says modestly, who can outrun his passes. As for defenses, the biggest block for a young pro quarterback, Harris always could recognize them. The big problem was learning to react, throwing the right pass quickly enough to take advantage of a situation.

It was that way with the Bills back in 1969, 1970, and 1971. He didn't make it then. But he took the frustration and disappointment of that experience and used them to re-evaluate his football career. If the opportunity ever came again, he decided, he'd be ready. Then whatever happened would happen.

When he joined the Rams he wasn't the same James Harris Buffalo had drafted on the fifth round in 1968. He had come to the Bills as a 22-year-old, knowing that he was a man under a microscope. His Grambling credentials were excellent—two championship teams, a couple of Orange Blossom classic victories.

When his team had played Morgan State in 1968 in New York's Yankee Stadium, 62,000 fans and a national television audience watched as he came off the bench with three minutes to play and drove his team to within inches of the winning touchdown, though badly hobbled by an injured ankle.

With rookie O. J. Simpson in his backfield, he started four games for Buffalo in 1969, then injured a knee and never started again the next two seasons. The club's indifference toward him hurt worse than sitting on the bench.

"I had the feeling it wouldn't have made a difference, no matter how well I played," he recalls. "That was hard to take. I called what I thought were good plays but they went nowhere. And when I did play, the club always was hopelessly behind and it was no secret that I was in there to pass.

"I wasn't ready for failure. I had been primed so long for a career in the NFL that I couldn't understand why it wasn't happening. And when I was cut just as the

James Harris took over as full-time starting quarterback for the Rams after John Hadl was traded.

1972 season was to begin, the club didn't tell me, a scout did. He just said the club didn't need me."

Harris tried other NFL teams with no luck. He was at rock bottom mentally and, figuring his career might be over, went to work for a government agency in Washington wondering, always wondering.

In Los Angeles, Rams owner Carroll Rosenbloom was wondering, too. Wondering what became of James Harris. He remembered some games in 1970 and 1971 when the Baltimore Colts, whom he owned at that time, had worked over Harris and how the youngster kept coming back.

Rams scout Tank Younger found Harris in Washington and signed him to a taxi squad contract for the remainder of 1972. Now it was up to Harris to prove in training camp that he could stick.

"I didn't realize until that camp that being idle had hurt so much," Harris says. "My timing was off, my arm was sore. I could hardly throw the ball, but they stuck with me."

His future turned in a preseason game against the NFL champion Dolphins. Los Angeles was winless in three games and trailed 17-0 after the first half. Harris came on and ignited the offense for a couple touchdowns. He didn't win the game but the Rams won their next eight, including the first six of the regular season.

"Looking back, I'd have to say that James showed us the way," Los Angeles coach Chuck Knox says.

That was his biggest contribution that season. He threw only 11 passes and wasn't expected to do much more in 1974. But the Rams were sluggish in winning just three of their first five games and Knox started Harris against the 49ers.

He completed 12 of 15 passes for 276 yards, including two for touchdowns and ran for a third score. A few hours later, Hadl was on his way to Green Bay. For the second time in his NFL career, Harris was number one.

The Rams coasted to the NFC West title and this time Harris showed that he belonged. In a game against Minnesota, he completed 10 straight passes in the fourth

James had an up-and-down three years with the Bills.

quarter to bring Los Angeles from a 17-6 deficit to a 20-17 victory. The winning score came on a pass to Jack Snow with 77 seconds to play.

In the first playoff game, he coolly guided the Rams past the Washington Redskins, a team famous for its cobweb-like pass defense. In the NFL playoff against the Vikings, the Rams were on the brink of breaking the game open when an offside penalty at the 1-yard line cost a touchdown. On the next play, Harris threw an interception.

No one holds that against him. He knows he belongs in the NFL, a long way from Monroe, Louisiana. That's where Robin-

son first saw him play and began trying to convince him to attend Grambling.

Other schools had similar ideas. At Michigan State, Duffy Daugherty talked to him about becoming a tight end. No thanks, Harris said. Another school said he would make a great wide receiver. Again, no thanks.

Robinson talked only of quarterback. And Harris listened. But no matter how well he played at Grambling, he still felt his chances in the NFL were at another position. Once he went to Robinson and asked if he could work at defensive back.

"Why?" his coach asked.

"Because that's where I think I might

His future with the Rams appears to be unlimited; he was named player of the game in the 1975 Pro Bowl game.

have to make it in the NFL," he replied.

"You're a quarterback here, you're going to stay at quarterback and you'll make it in the NFL as a quarterback," Robinson told him.

Through it all, Harris read every book Robinson gave him about playing quarterback. He watched films of NFL teams. And he paid attention. Once, Robinson recalls, Harris had his team on the 1-yard line on fourth down in a game against Jackson State. Robinson called the plays, but Harris asked his coach to call a quarterback rollout instead of a blast over the middle.

"The play lost ten yards but the big thing then was that James made a decision

on his own," Robinson says. "That's something every quarterback must learn. He never forgot that he had the choice but he never forgot that he made the wrong one, too."

All the quarterback training in the world would not really prepare him to face the pressure of being a black quarterback in the NFL. There were times in Buffalo when he felt a mistake would not only jeopardize his future but that of other blacks who came into pro football with the same aspirations.

Now all of that has passed. Other blacks, such as Joe Gilliam and Matthew Reed, have made successful starts, too.

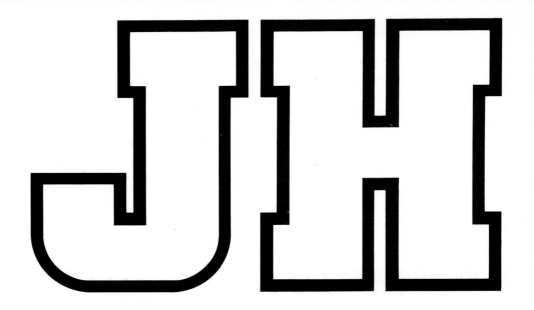

Jim Hart   St. Louis Cardinals

Jim Hart is unique among National Football League quarterbacks of the seventies —or sixties and fifties for that matter. He is the only full-time starter never to have been drafted, a free agent who defied the odds and beliefs that talented quarterbacks are easily spotted, hence quickly selected.

There have been other violations of that rule. Johnny Unitas, for instance. But even Unitas was a ninth-round draft choice of the Pittsburgh Steelers in 1955. He just wasn't reorganized until a year later.

But when Hart was eligible for the draft before the 1966 season, none of the 15 NFL or 9 AFL teams picked him. How could this happen? Even the St. Louis Cardinals, who ultimately signed him, and Hart himself are not sure. But in 1974 Jim led St. Louis to its first playoff since moving from Chicago in 1960—the first for any Cardinals team since 1948—and was named the NFC's most valuable player.

Until then, Hart had a roller-coaster career with rides from the taxi squad to number one, back down and up again. It wasn't until Don Coryell became head coach in 1973 that anyone flatly said Hart would be the number one quarterback —period.

That's part of the price of being a free agent, particularly a free agent quarterback. No one seems to want to believe that you are better than a quarterback who was drafted, particularly one who was drafted high. Jim has seen such men as Charley Johnson, Pete Beathard, and Gary Cuozzo come and go in St. Louis, always conceded a starting job ahead of him, yet never really matching his skills.

Jim Hart is not some Hollywood football story—the unknown from the little backwoods school who soared to glory, fame, fortune, and marries the pretty girl all within one reel.

It's taken him two reels.

He played at Southern Illinois and attracted many NFL scouts. In fact, he had been led to believe that he would be drafted because he filled out the standard questionnaires sent to likely draftees. Maybe it was his baby face or the team's bad season or the small college competition but it took a call from his coach, Don Shroyer, to get St. Louis interested. Shroyer had been an assistant with the Cardinals a few years earlier.

"I called and said that Jim was a great prospect," Shroyer says. "I told the Cardinals to sign him before someone else got lucky. He may not have had those great statistics that other college quarterbacks had but I started ten sophomores with him during his senior year. It seemed as if every time he passed he did it while he

was flat on his back."

A few days later the Cardinals signed Hart, gave him a small bonus, and told themselves he'd be just what they needed —someone to fill in for the likes of Buddy Humphrey, Terry Nofsinger, and Johnson when sore throwing arms accumulated in the early days of training camp.

Actually, Jim was one of five quarterbacks in that 1966 training camp. St. Louis had drafted Gary Snook from Iowa on the fourth round. Hart was very realistic about his situation—and about himself.

"I felt I could make the team," he says. "Of course I didn't know if I would. I figured that at least I'd enjoy the experience and if I was cut early, I'd have time to go somewhere else.

"As camp went along, I felt I was the better of the two rookies but I was hoping the money the Cardinals invested in Snook wouldn't enter into any final decisions."

It didn't. Jim was placed on the taxi squad for the season opener. That's when Johnson was called for army duty.

"Charley and I were walking home from practice early that week when he told me about his army duty," Hart recalls. "I was stunned. It seems everyone on the club knew but me. And the next day when Coach Winner told me I was the number one quarterback, I was stunned even more."

It was a gutsy decision by the Cardinals. There were veterans available for trade elsewhere in the NFL but they decided Hart would be their man. For one season, Johnson would be available for each game and the team expected him to return to fulltime play within two seasons. The Cardinals also had begun to see Jim's potential.

"Coach told me that he could try to trade for a veteran but felt that I had the arm, the release, the potential, everything to be a top quarterback," Hart says.

"We really wanted someone to build on, to grow with," Winner says. "Jimmy had improved tremendously though he still threw a lot of interceptions. But the decision really wasn't that hard at the time. I just told him he was our number one quarterback and that we were going with him

all the way. He had the ability. We just didn't know if that ability was ready to come out yet."

It did. Hart gained 3,008 yards that season but set a club record with 30 interceptions as the Cardinals finished with a 6-7-1

Jim Hart is the only full-time starting quarterback in the NFL who was signed as a free agent.

record. The next season, with Johnson still in the army, the Cards missed a division title by half a game.

Jim had cut his interceptions to 18 and had begun to impress NFL coaches. What they liked most was his ability to throw the deep square-out pass, probably the most difficult pass to throw accurately.

Hart could pass. Many felt he was superior to Johnson, who had suffered shoulder and arm miseries during his career. The two split the quarterbacking in 1969 after Hart injured a finger in training camp. Neither was happy with this situation and after the season, Johnson asked to be traded. The Cardinals obliged.

Hart was number one again and on the way to a division title in 1970 until the team blew a three-game lead in the last half of the season and finished third. As usual when fans become disgruntled, the quarterback takes the brunt of their criticism.

Bob Hollway, for several seasons the defensive coach at Minnesota, became Cardinals head coach in 1971. Hollway then obtained Gary Cuozzo from the Vikings. Cuozzo, he said, would be the number one quarterback, Beathard would be number two, and Hart number three. None of the Cardinals' fans seemed to mind because they could not forget—nor forgive—the shock of seeing their team crumble the previous season.

Hart felt the stings most of all, even after Cuozzo and Beathard failed to work out. In a home game against Philadelphia, he was pounded to the ground and lay motionless. The trainers wheeled him off the field on a stretcher with a severe concussion and the Busch Stadium crowd cheered—his injury, not him.

In the next home game against Green Bay, all the Cardinals needed to win was for Hart to fall down with each center snap and allow the clock to run out. Two Packers time outs, a penalty, and a decision by Hollway to call an ill-fated sweep on fourth down forced St. Louis to give up the ball with enough time for the Packers to get a tie-making field goal.

Hart was booed.

It wasn't until 1974 that the cheers in Busch Stadium were really positive. Don Coryell had come as head coach in 1973 and told Hart he would be the number one quarterback. So it was back up to the top of the roller coaster again.

"There was no question that Jim would be number one," Coryell says. "The first time we looked at Cardinals films it was

Coach Don Coryell assured Jim that he would be the number one quarterback.

apparent that he had the best arm and now he's proved to have all the other assets that a great quarterback needs.

"He doesn't throw interceptions, he's a very good field leader . . . very calm, very cool."

Hart cut his interceptions to eight and threw 20 touchdowns in helping St. Louis to its NFC East title in 1974. Coryell, who favored the pass over the run when he came to the Cardinals, gave him a more balanced attack with the running of Terry Metcalf. That helped, too.

Just a year before, there was some doubt whether Hart's career was over. He had suffered a hyperextended elbow when hit attempting to pass and missed the final two games. Doctors, unwilling to risk surgery, ordered complete rest and therapy. Often he slept with an ice pack on the elbow, but to no avail.

Pain lingered and doctors worried. Again there was talk of surgery but because the surgeons feared his career might be endangered, Hart stayed with the rest and therapy program. Finally in the spring of 1974, the program was successful and his arm was good as new.

Perhaps Jim Hart's career really was one great risk because he's done what no other recent free agent quarterback coming directly from college has done.

His secret for such unusual success?

"Nothing magical," he says. "When I went to that first training camp, I was determined to learn as much as possible. When I became a number two quarterback, I made myself be patient and continue learning . . . none of that 'I want to play or be traded' business.

"I had an awful lot to learn, particularly about reading defenses and setting up quicker in the pocket. My maturity in pro football has come from being able to recognize the defenses . . . and I'm still working on setting up faster, though I set up as well as most and a lot better than some of the so-called great quarterbacks."

Jim is blessed with great natural talent.

He shows quick wrist snap and good follow-through.

51

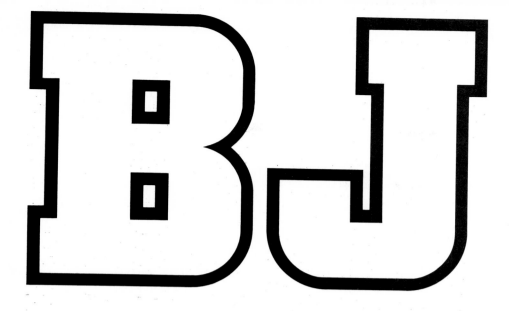

Bert Jones   Baltimore Colts

In horse racing, breeding means a lot. The best example is Secretariat, who won the Triple Crown in 1973 and was acclaimed by many as the greatest thoroughbread horse of all time. What made him a champion, the experts said, were the qualities—speed, heart, and endurance—that he had inherited from his daddy, Bold Ruler, also a great horse in his time.

Maybe it's the same with football players. In Baltimore, the Colts have put a good part of their future into the hands of young quarterback Bert Jones. His dad is Dub Jones, who was a star running back and receiver on Paul Brown's great Cleveland Browns teams.

There never is any guarantee that such success will be passed on in the same measure—either in horse racing or football.

Bert Jones is like a young thoroughbred. His training still isn't finished and won't be until he has four or five seasons of competition. It is then that he'll be expected to go out and prove that he is a champion.

People in the National Football League who know talent predicted that would happen even before he joined the Colts as a number one draft choice in 1973. At that time, Baltimore had torn apart a veteran team that had been so successful throughout the sixties and had begun to build with inexperienced, young players.

Jones is the keystone in Baltimore's rebuilding. Joe Thomas, the Colts' general manager who ordered the demolition of a veteran team and supervises the reconstruction, says he wouldn't trade Bert for any quarterback in the NFL. That is not idle talk. When the Colts had the first pick in the 1975 draft, Thomas traded it to Atlanta for all-pro offensive tackle George Kunz. They also got a first round selection in return, which Thomas used to select an All-America guard, Ken Huff of North Carolina.

"We had to start giving Bert some help," Thomas says. "The worst thing that can happen to a young quarterback is that he takes such a fearful pounding and becomes gun-shy. We want him to develop in comparative safety."

Jones has the ability to go from there. He came into the NFL knowing what life would be like because he had watched other young players endure the growing process when his father was an assistant coach at Cleveland before moving the family to Louisiana. Yet it was up to Bert to do it on his own.

At Ruston High School in Louisiana, Bert was a good quarterback. But no matter what he did, it didn't seem to compare with a kid named Joe Ferguson who played in Freeport, about 70 miles away. A great rivalry grew between the two and exists today when Baltimore and the Buffalo Bills play each other.

"Joe was Mr. Everything, I was Mr. Nothing," Jones remembers, chuckling at the oversimplification. "But I always felt that I had as much ability as he did, and more. The difference was that he threw the ball a lot in high school, I didn't. And he had a better team around him than I did."

College coaches, including Charley McClendon of LSU, fell over each other trying to recruit Ferguson. Joe finally decided to attend Arkansas. So LSU went after Jones. But Bert admits that even had Ferguson decided on LSU, he still would have gone to the school.

Notre Dame was another school interested in Jones. Ara Parseghian and Dub Jones had been roommates on the Browns and Bert could have sought a scholarship had he wished.

"I like to hunt and fish too much to leave Louisiana so I decided I'd go to school near my home," he says.

Jones did not have an easy time of it at LSU. As a sophomore, he required knee surgery. Then he spent most of his junior year as a backup quarterback. But when he had finished his senior year, even with that limited playing time, he owned 20 school passing records, some dating back a quarter century to Y. A. Tittle.

Pro scouts long before had been alerted to his talent. Many knew him personally because of his father's football work so there rarely has been a player scouted so thoroughly.

What they liked—and what they felt would make him an excellent NFL quarterback—was his size at 6 foot 3 inches, 205 pounds, the range of his arm, an extraordinarily quick release, and his ability to work so relaxed from the pocket—in other words, a classic pro passer.

Maybe it's his breeding, too, but those who watch him are impressed with his ability to step into a huddle and command

Bert Jones spent one year at LSU as a backup quarterback, but he held 20 school passing records when he finished.

a team. Like Ken Stabler at Oakland, he appears to be overly cocky. He's not, just filled with confidence.

There was a game at LSU against bitter rival Mississippi. Ole Miss led 16-10 with three minutes to play when Jones got the ball at his 20-yard line. He completed three of four passes and, with one second to play, called time out at Mississippi's 10-yard line. He walked over to talk to McClendon.

"This is it," his coach warned him, after suggesting a swing pass to halfback Brad Davis.

"Don't worry," Jones told his coach, "I'll get it."

He did just that. Davis caught the ball and raced into the end zone as time expired. The extra point gave LSU a 17-16 victory.

Call that cool. And Jones has plenty.

"I've always felt that football, especially for a quarterback, is a thinking man's game," he says. "I don't think you can play if you're nervous.

"As a rookie with the Colts, I went through an orientation program. I got myself relaxed, felt much more poised in my second year and there were few times that I didn't know what was happening . . . why I did this or did that."

The immediate impression always is that the son of a former great player gets this way because he is force-fed a football diet from the day he takes his first bottle. Nothing is further from the truth in the Jones house.

"I spent a few summers as a youngster at the Browns' training camp," Bert recalls. "I used to warm up the veteran quarterbacks before practice but I could see what the rookies were going through, too. My dad was very understanding about their situation and he took time to explain what was happening anytime I asked."

Jones stressed that phrase, "anytime I asked." His father never pushed him or any of his brothers to become football players. But he never hesitated to teach them the game's fundamentals or fine points, if asked. He once told Bert he didn't care whether he went out for the high school band or the football team, provided he gave either choice his best effort.

"Playing football was something I wanted to do," he says. "I guess what he had done was always an incentive to me. I went through the 'He's-Dub Jones's-son' routine at LSU and I accepted it.

"But when my brother Ben went to LSU after I did, he had to listen to, 'He's Bert Jones's brother.' That made me feel good."

There also was a measure of satisfaction in having a father who totally understood the problems of playing with a team that was starting from scratch, as Jones did his first two seasons.

"He was a good guy to talk to," Bert admits. "I guess I had unique parental guidance. We'd talk over why certain things didn't work and he'd enlighten me. What it boiled down to was him telling me, 'Today is today, things will get better tomorrow.' That helped a lot."

In Baltimore, Bert has a magnetic appeal. He is dark-haired, good-looking, with a warm, country-boy personality. Those around the Colts marvel at how people flock to him—outsiders and teammates as well.

"If Baltimore needed someone to hold the fort until help came, Bert Jones couldn't have been a better choice," says Ernie Accorsi, a former Colts' official and now a member of NFL commissioner Pete Rozelle's staff.

Jones took a pounding during the building process. As a rookie, Howard Schnellenberger, the Colts' head coach, gave him more playing time during that preseason than Marty Domres, the holdover number one quarterback. It looked like a wise move when the team won two preseason games with Jones.

As a starter though, he couldn't produce a victory in the first five games and was benched, never to start again that season. The only time he played was when Baltimore got far behind and Schnellenberger needed a passer.

Jones knew about pro football's learning process as applied to rookie quarterbacks. But as he sat on the Colts' bench during the remainder of the 1973 season, his patience and understanding dimmed because he saw that Domres was not performing any better.

Bert has confidence in his ability to step into a huddle and take command. He does, too.

That problem was settled early in the 1974 season when Joe Thomas took the head coaching job and immediately made Jones number one quarterback for the rest of that season. Bert got a victory over Joe Namath and the New York Jets the first time the two met, then missed four games because of an injured shoulder.

In the final game against the Jets, he lost a wild 45-38 game to Namath but set an NFL record of 17 consecutive completions. There were two bits of irony in that game. When the Namath-Jones duel ended, Jones had thrown twice as many passes. He completed 36 of 53 for 385 yards and four touchdowns; Namath had 19 of 28 for 281 yards and two touchdowns.

The pass that broke Ken Anderson's record of 16 consecutive completions wound up losing yardage, the only time all day that particular play broke down. And what would have been an eighteenth consecutive completion was dropped!

Bert Jones never said a word when that happened. That is part of his championship breeding, too.

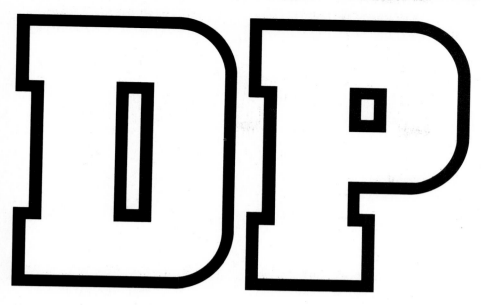

Dan Pastorini   Houston Oilers

Mean Joe Greene, the massive defensive tackle of the Pittsburgh Steelers, sat in the visiting team's dressing room in the Astrodome one Sunday a few years ago, and shook his head sadly.

"I really feel sorry for that Pastorini kid," he said. "He's going to get killed. He just can't go on like that. He's got more guts than any quarterback I've ever seen but he needs more than guts."

Greene and the Steelers had manhandled the Houston Oilers, sacking quarterback Dan Pastorini nine times. Even some of the Steelers' other defensive linemen admitted they began to feel badly about pounding and harassing the young quarterback so freely.

That was a mere sampling of the first few seasons in the National Football League for dark, dashing Dante Anthony Pastorini, who looks as if he stepped from a Hollywood movie lot. To the time that Greene & Company visited Houston, his only professional moment of glory had been in 1971 when he was the third player picked in the draft. From that day until the 1974 season concluded with a respectable 7-7 record, his pro career had suffered.

There were two seasons in which the Oilers won just one game and lost 13. Three football coaches preached their own particular football philosophy within four years. Players came and went as if Houston's dressing room was just a way station.

Through it all, Pastorini fumed and fretted, totally frustrated at the lack of success. The more he fumed, the less he accomplished with his teammates; the more he fretted, the less he accomplished for himself; the more frustrated he became, the more he inhibited his own abilities.

He since has matured on the job. He no longer belittles his teammates' efforts but inspires them to be better. And they respond. His talents, held in such high regard the day he was drafted, have flowered and many feel he may surpass the other two quarterbacks drafted ahead of him in 1971—New England's Jim Plunkett and New Orleans's Archie Manning.

Through the turmoil that marked Pastorini's early seasons in the NFL, one fact never has changed. There is not a quarterback who can throw a football further with seemingly less effort.

That's the easy part. To get a clear picture of Dan Pastorini, one must go back to his youth when the idea of becoming a professional athlete really sharpened his focus on the future.

He watched pro athletes on television. When he went to Bellarmine High School in San Jose, California, and later to Santa Clara University, he concentrated on foot-

ball and baseball because he wanted to play them professionally.

His early heroes were Bart Starr, Johnny Unitas, and, because he lived just an hour's drive from San Francisco's Candlestick Park, outfielder Willie Mays of the Giants. When Mays wound up his career with the New York Mets, Pastorini well might have been his successor in center field had he accepted the team's offer to turn pro after an excellent career as a high school outfielder.

But he turned to pro football.

"Bart Starr really was my idol," Pastorini admits. "When I was a rookie I met him in Houston and he was just as I always imagined he would be. He said some real nice things to me, gave me some good advice, and I really choked up a bit thinking he would take time to do that.

"The best part is that I still hear from him. He drops me a note a couple of times a year. When I finish playing in the NFL, I want to look back and be able to say I did as much as he did."

No one doubted that he could have his football career.

Instead of picking a big-time college to build his talent, he chose Santa Clara, a small college 50 miles south of San Francisco.

Pastorini could have gone to almost any school in the country—USC, UCLA, Notre Dame—they all wanted him. But he chose Santa Clara for one reason—Pat Malley, the football coach.

His brother Butch had played for Malley, who several times refused to allow the older Pastorini to play when sick or injured. His regard for a person over winning made an impression on Dan. So did Malley's recruiting speech.

"If you come to Santa Clara," he told Pastorini, "you'll get what you earn. I'm not going to give you anything on a silver platter."

That was in stark contrast to the other recruiters' pitches and it's what sold him.

"When I got out of Santa Clara, I was a better person than when I went in. I owe

Mean Joe Greene once said that Dan Pastorini "has more guts than any quarterback I've ever seen."

that to Pat Malley because he made me a better man than football player," Pastorini says.

But Dan also had saddled himself with a challenge because of his choice of schools. Nearby was Stanford where Jim Plunkett received the publicity—and ultimately the Heisman trophy—while every nice thing said about Pastorini always ended with ". . . but he plays for a small college."

That bothered him.

Everywhere he went he heard that Plunkett was better, that playing on a major college level gave Jim a better chance in professional football. Pastorini didn't like it.

His small college background—he was a Little All-America quarterback—didn't diminish the enthusiasm of NFL scouts. When the 1971 draft came, the three top-rated quarterbacks were Plunkett, Manning, and Pastorini and they were the first three players picked, in that order.

The only drawback, the scouts said of Pastorini, was that it may take him a bit longer to become an accomplished pro quarterback because of his small-college background.

That burned him then—and still does—because he never doubted his ability.

"Success for any quarterback in football is getting the ball into the end zone," he says. "That is the equal factor at all levels. I could have played in the same kind of competition as Plunkett and Manning but I chose not to. That didn't mean I would be less of an NFL quarterback."

At 6 foot 3 inches and 205 pounds, he had the ideal size and strength for the position. Those qualities came in handy during his early seasons because he'd be forced to take quite a pounding. From those misfortunes, he developed a knack of using those dimensions to some advantage.

Late in the 1971 season at Buffalo, Houston trailed the Bills 14-13 with a minute to play. On a fourth-and-six play, he searched for a receiver but could find none open. Eager Buffalo arms wrapped around his legs and middle, dragging him down.

With his knees just inches from the ground, he suddenly saw wide receiver Jim Beirne left uncovered and he threw.

"I never have been able to accept defeat," says Dan.

Beirne caught the ball, ran to the 6-yard line, and two plays later the Oilers scored the winning touchdown. That victory began a three game, season-ending winning streak.

But the winning streak and personal exploits were brief skyrocket rides which quickly fizzled over the next couple of seasons. Pastorini's trouble was not so much trying to read enemy defenses as it was controlling his own emotions when those around him faltered.

On one hand there was the challenge of being a quarterback. To him it was an achievement to get 10 other players to do as he directed, to listen to what he'd been taught and believe what he wanted done was right and should be done.

He saw this as his job. At the same time, that belief ran into one of his own basic rules.

"I have never been able to accept defeat in any way," he says. "It is degrading, demoralizing, disgusting, embarrassing. I work too hard to lose and so do the other players who give the game their best efforts."

Once, after a loss to Atlanta in his second season, he sounded off for all to hear and read.

"There are a lot of guys on this team who don't want to play football," he said. "We won't become a good football team until these players are gone. Some of them shouldn't even be playing in the NFL."

Such criticism didn't set well with his teammates. It wasn't until the Oilers brought in King Hill as an assistant coach that Pastorini began to settle down. One of the first things Hill, a former NFL quarterback, got Pastorini to admit was that Dan was his own worst enemy in not controlling his emotions and harnessing his talent.

"That guy is so great," Pastorini says. "First, he made me see what a fool I was making of myself with all that talk. Then he got me to look at myself from a different point of view, mainly that I wasn't helping the team or myself by doing all of this.

"He didn't try to make me less competitive, only to try to steer those instincts in a positive manner. Once I did that, my game

Dan scrambles to evade a diving tackle attempt by Vikings' defensive tackle Doug Sutherland.

began to come around."

The first indication came in 1974 when, after missing the preseason and most of the first half of the regular season with an injury, Pastorini returned and the Oilers won six of their last eight games.

"You could see the difference," one coach said. "The whole team had a different feeling. Dan himself looked like a veteran, not a kid. He didn't get rattled when things went wrong in a game. He even kept himself under control in prac-

tice if things got messed up."

Pastorini also has learned to use the strength in his arm. Early in his career, he was "bomb happy." Now he has become adept at the short pass and still can throw deep when he must.

To Pastorini, his career is just beginning. Ahead lie hopes of winning the Super Bowl, of someday entering the Hall of Fame, "and of playing well enough that people will remember me, just like I remember Bart Starr."

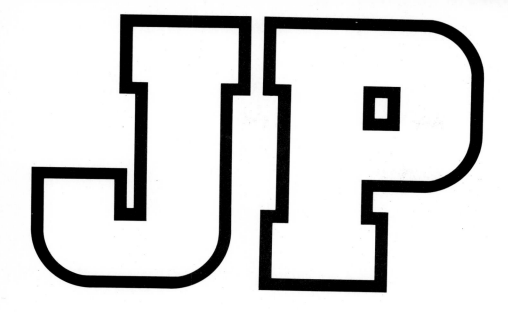

Jim Plunkett   San Francisco 49ers

There is a certain charisma about a football player who wins the Heisman trophy. He is supposed to be the best college football player in the country, a superstar among superstars . . . maybe even a player who can turn losers into winners just by showing up.

In the NFL draft, Heisman trophy winners almost always are high selections. Some, such as O. J. Simpson and Jim Plunkett, have even greater distinction. They were the first players picked in their drafts.

Plunkett is a quarterback, the most important offensive player on any pro team. And if there was one player the New England Patriots truly needed when the 1971 draft began, it was a quarterback.

In 1970, the Patriots won just 2 of 14 games, which was the reason they had the first pick. Joe Kapp, the quarterback that year, had failed to produce the same magic that helped the Minnesota Vikings to the Super Bowl the previous season. What the team really needed was a star, a leader.

The Patriots sought someone with great football breeding, someone around whom they could build their future.

Almost everyone agreed Plunkett was that player. He had broken every major passing record at Stanford University during three great seasons, won the Heisman

trophy as a senior, then helped beat undefeated Ohio State in the Rose Bowl. His success came from ability, tough competition and good coaching by John Ralston, former NFL head coach Jack Christiansen —an assistant at Stanford—and San Francisco 49ers quarterback John Brodie.

To the Patriots, losers for four consecutive seasons, Plunkett indeed seemed to be the answer. As a rookie, he engineered some astounding upsets . . . the mighty Oakland Raiders in the season opener . . . the soon-to-be AFC champion Miami Dolphins . . . and the reigning NFL champion Baltimore Colts, a loss that cost the Colts the AFC East title in the season's final game.

Plunkett and the Patriots won six games that first season, as many as the team had managed the previous two seasons combined. In New England, he made Boston's Big Three—baseball's Carl Yastrzemski, basketball's John Havlicek, and hockey's Bobby Orr—move over to make a Big Four.

Few quarterbacks ever began their professional careers in such fashion. But it was to become the measure of Plunkett's ability and character that he could survive a couple of struggling seasons thereafter and still maintain the promise predicted for him.

Those who know Plunkett find him an

Jim took a great physical beating carrying the ball his first year. He'll still run when he can.

He reads plays beautifully, waiting the extra half second and then hitting the wide receiver breaking into the clear.

extraordinary person. After the cruelest or most one-sided defeats, he faces questioners and doesn't flinch. He's the same after games in which he does not play well as he is in those in which he is spectacular or in games in which he plays well but is betrayed by the mistakes of others.

There is an inner strength to Plunkett that keeps him from total defeat, though he may be battered and dejected at times.

It could come from the fact he was raised by parents who were blind. His father supported his family as a news vendor in the post office in San Jose, California, until he died when Jim was 21.

When Jim was 18 years old, doctors discovered a thyroid tumor deep in the left side of his neck that threatened his life. Fortunately the tumor was not serious and all it cost Plunkett was a couple of weeks of practice with Stanford's freshman football team.

Football had become a part of his life when he was in the fifth grade and, "When I found out I could throw in the eighth grade," he became a quarterback and led his team to the county championship. At James Lick High School in San Jose, his teams won championships in his junior and senior years. But when he played for the North in California's North-South all-star game, it was as a defensive end. Mike Holmgren, who would play for USC, quarterbacked the North that day.

College recruiters flocked to Plunkett but he chose Stanford because it was near his home and he could keep close contact with his parents. The school also had an excellent scholastic reputation and provided an ideal showcase for his football talent.

Plunkett did not play as a sophomore and became eligible for the NFL draft following his second year of varsity competition. Many thought he would forego his final year of eligibility at Stanford. That wasn't Jim's way.

"If I had left," he says, "I always would have felt that I let down the team before our goals were reached. We were telling kids then not to drop out, to finish school, to set targets and to work around them. What would they have thought if I had dropped out for professional football?"

He stayed and the goals—a Pacific-8 championship and Rose Bowl victory—were achieved. Plunkett completed 20 of 30 passes in Stanford's 27-17 upset of Ohio State in the Rose Bowl. Adding it up, he had his Heisman trophy . . . his Pacific-8 title . . . his Rose Bowl victory . . . his education . . . and now he was ready for the NFL.

It appeared in 1971 that the NFL wasn't quite ready for him. He got those six victories, was named rookie of the year, and became the first rookie quarterback to play every offensive down. For the most part, he passed with the poise of a veteran, called his own plays, and was a leader far in excess of his years.

To Plunkett, there was nothing magical about his rookie season.

He took it all in stride, as he always did. To him, being the number one draft pick in the NFL meant nothing more than his reason for being there. He did not ask for special privileges. He had no tantrums. He never said we-did-it-this-way-at-Stanford.

He communicated, not only in football terms, but in general. He'd sit down and talk with the most intelligent people on the team and then he'd move on and be just as much at home with those men who didn't fall into that category.

This carried over onto the field. He gave the team what it needed—character.

"He instilled some backbone instead of wishbone," one of his coaches says.

That was on the surface. He made mistakes that first season, more than a few. For instance, in one preseason game, he leaned into the huddle and called "Green Forty-two."

"I remembered we had no such play when I got to the line of scrimmage," he recalls with a laugh. "That was a Stanford play but it was the only one I could think of. We ran something or other and still made some yardage."

In a regular season game, he had eight running plays in his game plan but called only four.

"I forgot the rest," he admits.

John Mazur, then coach of the Patriots and himself a former quarterback, had decided to keep things as simple as possible for Plunkett. For example, Jim didn't have to watch for blitzing linebackers and then call audibles. It was automatic that a back's first responsibility was to check for a blitz before running a pattern.

"I was on a three-year plan then," he says. "They told me they didn't want a polished quarterback as soon as possible but one who got better each week. Everything was kept simple and they let me go my own way pretty much."

Only when he got into serious trouble would the coaches come to his rescue. In some games, Mazur never sent in a play. Over the season, he never sent in more than five in any one game. Plunkett says he matured faster as a result.

He paid a fearful price that season and for a couple thereafter. Even at Stanford, Plunkett was not reluctant to run if he saw no hope on a pass pattern. Opposing defenses in the NFL gladly piled into him.

"I took a physical beating I'll always remember, carrying the ball my first year," he says ruefully.

His pass protection was something less than great during his first three seasons; his ability to avoid interceptions the same. In three years, he was sacked 112 times and threw 58 interceptions, 25 of those in his second season, when everything seemed to go wrong.

In fact, Plunkett was dejected and confused at the end of that second season, when the team won just three games. Trouble between the coaching staff and front office and disciplinary problems divided the team.

To make matters worse, Plunkett played with bruised ribs and torn cartilage in his chest early in the year; he later hurt his shoulder and with three games to go he tore a cartilage in his left knee (the right one had surgery when he was at Stanford). Just when he thought the knee was healing, he injured it stepping from his car and required surgery.

None of that has changed his style. All changes have come through experience and some extra hard knocks. Plunkett still will run with the ball if his pass protection breaks down or if he feels he can make

more by running.

He found a receiver in former Stanford teammate Randy Vataha, who in a football uniform looks like one of the Seven Dwarfs he used to imitate when he worked at Disneyland. Because they knew each other's football habits so well, the two teamed many times on crucial touchdowns or big plays that kept scoring drives going.

There's a lot of bodies around the football as Jim scores a touchdown against the Baltimore Colts.

Plunkett is adept at throwing on the run; he's strong enough (6 feet 2 inches and 205 pounds) to stand in the pocket and throw the ball while being tackled. Defensive linemen often had his jersey stretched, trying to haul him down, only to have him complete his pass anyway.

In the spring of 1976, Jim Plunkett traded uniforms, switching from the red, white, and blue of the Patriots to the scarlet and gold of the San Francisco 49ers. Plunkett had asked that he be traded to San Francisco so he could be closer to his blind mother. The 49ers paid a high price for Plunkett—quarterback Tom Owen, three first-round draft choices, and a second-round selection. Quarterbacks of Plunkett's quality aren't often available.

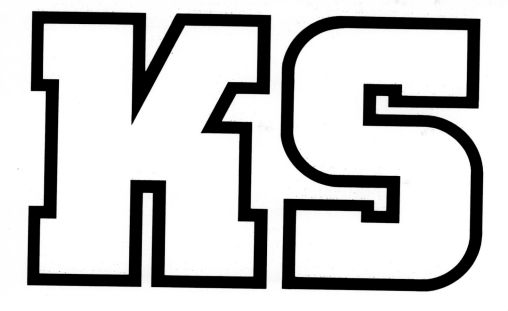

Ken Stabler   Oakland Raiders

There were 35 seconds to play in a 1974 American Football Conference playoff game in Oakland's Coliseum. The Miami Dolphins, looking to return to the Super Bowl for the fourth year in a row and perhaps become the first team ever to win three Super Bowls in a row, held a 26-21 lead over the Oakland Raiders.

These teams were supposed to be the best in the National Football League. Some had called the game "the real Super Bowl," and both had played as if it was the Super Bowl. The Dolphins had gone ahead for the fourth time that afternoon with about two minutes to play.

But the Raiders were far from beaten —and they advanced the ball to Miami's 8-yard line. So often in the past, this was a time for ageless George Blanda, Oakland's great placekicker. But Blanda's foot couldn't win the game now. It was left to quarterback Ken Stabler, who already had thrown three touchdown passes.

As soon as center Jim Otto snapped the ball, Stabler dropped back to pass, his left arm cocked, waiting for one of his black-jerseyed receivers to break free in the end zone. His eyes searched the area frantically but every Raider was shadowed by at least two defenders.

Stabler looked again, knowing that a wall of Dolphins defensive linemen was closing in. Still no one came open and Miami defensive end Vern Den Herder crashed against Ken's ankles. His feet were being pulled from beneath him and his only option was to throw a pass to a receiver cutting across the end zone, no matter how many Dolphins were with him.

Instinctively he lofted the ball, hoping the intended receiver could leap higher than his defenders or at least bat the ball away from a possible interception. Without realizing it, he had chosen the smallest Oakland player, 5-foot 10-inch Clarence Davis. Davis leaped high in the air and got his hands on the ball before two Miami defenders could react.

Stabler couldn't see this struggle because Den Herder had sent him crashing to the ground. But he heard 54,000 voices in the Coliseum roar. Then he saw Davis holding the ball aloft and an official next to him signaling: Touchdown!

There were 26 seconds left to play.

In the nine seconds since he had taken Otto's center snap, it seemed that Ken Stabler's life had flashed before his eyes. For the first time since 1968, when he was a second-round draft pick, Ken Stabler felt the special glow of a great achievement with the Oakland Raiders.

There had been other notable moments

and once, two years before, there was that same glow—briefly. That was in another AFC playoff game, in Pittsburgh. Stabler had relieved Daryle Lamonica with Oakland trailing 6-0 and ran 30 yards for a touchdown with less than 90 seconds to play.

But that day belonged to Terry Bradshaw and Franco Harris. It was the day of the "immaculate reception," when Harris caught a deflected fourth-down pass and ran for the winning touchdown.

What happened in Pittsburgh that day tells the story of Stabler—and the Raiders—since 1968. Ken was drafted only a couple of weeks after Super Bowl II, when Oakland was beaten by Green Bay. But the Raiders were conceded to be the best team in the American Football League at that time, and many felt they were destined to play in many Super Bowls.

Something always happened. For the next three years, the Raiders won their division and lost in the AFC playoffs. They didn't make the playoffs in 1971, then won three more division titles and lost again in the playoffs each time.

Even after that victory over Miami in 1974, the Raiders were beaten easily the following week by Pittsburgh and the

"I'm able to counteract any defense now," says Ken Stabler. "I'm totally at home and in command on the field."

Steelers went on to win the Super Bowl.

The misfortune that has dogged Oakland during this time also has dogged Stabler. In his rookie season, he did a good job in a preseason scrimmage against the Dallas rookies. Then he re-injured a knee that had bothered him at Alabama. Oakland sent him to Spokane of the Continental Football League to work himself into shape but the knee was so bad he had to have surgery.

In 1969, personal problems at home caused him to walk out of the Raiders' training camp. He came back in 1970 ready to give pro football a full shot. All that meant was serving as a backup to Lamonica and Blanda. He played very little.

But Stabler was not idle. Often he would sit or stand next to Blanda and ask him about what was happening in the game —and, most importantly, why. Some days he would call the game from the bench and have Blanda critique each play selection in light of what happened on the field.

This went on for three seasons. Many young quarterbacks would have become frustrated and disenchanted at not playing and probably would have asked to be traded to a team where they could play.

Not Stabler.

"The Raiders were winning in those years and I shared in the rewards," he says. "I learned the system thoroughly, so thoroughly in fact, I'm able now to counteract any defense. I'm totally at home and in command on the field."

That's not to say he was satisfied not playing. He was the starting quarterback when the 1972 season opened in Pittsburgh but had a bad game and didn't start again that season. He remembers the day in 1973 when the Raiders broke Miami's winning streak at 18 games. The only thing he did that day was hold for Blanda's kicks.

"Everyone was happy we won and that we broke Miami's winning streak—everyone, I guess, but me," Ken recalls.

"Sitting on the bench was getting to be a drag. That night I just moped around, unhappy on a day when everyone in Oakland was sitting on top of the world."

But pro football was changing and Lamonica, for one, could not adapt to the changes. Daryle had been nicknamed the "Mad Bomber" because he thrived on long passes that were so much a part of the Raiders' offense. With the advent of more zone defenses, such passes became obsolete.

Oakland's record was 1-1 with that victory over Miami but the offense had done little. The following week against Kansas City it still floundered and Raiders coach John Madden called for Stabler. Ken couldn't produce a victory but he had become a startling quarterback.

Just a year before, he had told a friend, "I'm twenty-seven years old and it's time to be what I'm going to be. I wouldn't be worth anything to myself, the Raiders or anyone else if I didn't feel I could make the grade."

Now he had. In his first four games as a starter, he got three wins and a tie. In the fifth game, against Baltimore, he was doubtful because of a sprained ankle and dislocated toe. Yet he completed 25 of 29 passes for 304 yards. It was the most efficient performance, under the NFL's rating system, by any quarterback since a Sammy Baugh game for the Washington Redskins in 1945—2½ months before Ken Stabler was born.

When the 1973 season ended, Stabler was rated the best passer in the AFC. When the 1974 season ended, he was named its most valuable player.

Most people say that Stabler has made it now but success hasn't changed him. On the field he always had looked confident whether he had plenty of time to throw or was fighting the clock and the Miami Dolphins as in that 1974 playoff game.

To know Stabler one must distinguish between cockiness and confidence. Ken always is confident, so sure of what he'll do because of his long years of preparation, first at Alabama, then on the Oakland bench.

A good example came in 1974 against the Cincinnati Bengals. Trailing 27-23, the Raiders got the ball at their 48-yard line with 96 seconds to play but without any time outs. Stabler completed four con-

secutive passes and got to the Bengals' 1-yard line with 30 seconds to play. A running play failed and he quickly threw the ball away to stop the clock. On the next play, Charlie Smith swept into the right corner of the end zone for the winning touchdown—and still there were eight seconds left.

He walked away from that game as if it had been another day at practice. That is the mark of a great athlete and Stabler always has been that, right from his high school days in Foley, Alabama. It was there as a freshman that he acquired the nickname "Snake," after running back a punt 70 yards for a touchdown.

"To get the seventy yards," he says, "I must have zig-zagged three hundred."

In basketball as in football, he was all-state—and was a good enough left-handed pitcher to receive a huge bonus offer from the Houston Astros. But football was his first love and, even though he had been a great Auburn fan as a youngster, he accepted a scholarship offer from the Tigers' archrival, Alabama.

Only because of Bear Bryant, whom Stabler still praises.

"I can't explain how much of an effect Bear had on my life," Ken says. "He probably meant more to me than any person I can name. He instilled in me things like leadership, accepting praise, and criticism, and a willingness to sacrifice."

Stabler was a freshman when Joe Namath was a senior at Alabama but when Ken graduated, Bryant said that Ken was the best quarterback ever to play for him.

For good reason. Alabama had a 19-2-1 record in the two seasons Stabler was quarterback. He was named most valuable player of the 1967 Sugar Bowl after his team routed Nebraska 34-7.

The year before, Stabler was quite a scrambler and led the team in rushing. But a knee injury curtailed his running as a senior and forced him to concentrate on throwing from the pocket. He says now that it made him a better passer, the key for any successful NFL quarterback.

Ken keeps his eyes on his receiver, and not on the mad charge of onrushing Steelers' tackle Joe Greene.

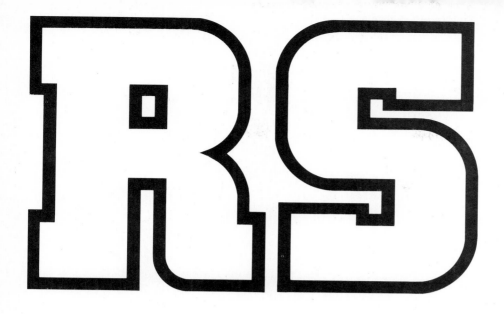

Roger Staubach   Dallas Cowboys

It was Tom Landry's rule of thumb that a quarterback required five seasons of National Football League competition before becoming established and competent. Note the past tense "was" because that predated Roger Staubach's coming to play for Landry and the Dallas Cowboys in 1969.

Had Landry stubbornly stuck by that rule, the five-season period would have expired in 1973 and he might not be able to look back on:

—Winning Super Bowl VI in January 1972.

—Making the finals of the 1972 NFC playoffs after a narrow victory over San Francisco.

—Making the finals of the 1973 NFC playoffs after another close call against the Los Angeles Rams.

In all three instances, the man behind the center was Roger Staubach. They called him Roger the Dodger during his All-America days at Navy when, as a junior, he danced and passed his way to the Heisman trophy and into the Cotton Bowl. He's also the same Roger Staubach who showed up at the Cowboys' training camp as a 27-year old rookie and caused many to say he'd never make it because he had been away from top-flight competition for four years.

Three seasons later, he was not only

quarterback of the Super Bowl champions, but the game's most valuable player. That caused Landry to revise his theory about quarterbacks making it in the NFL—a revision that Landry steadfastly applies only to Staubach.

Why Staubach? Landry always has considered him a special talent. He likes his quarterbacks serious, devoted to the job, and willing to adhere to intricate game plans. And he likes them strong-armed, quick-thinking, and athletically sound.

Staubach, in contrast to the team's other two quarterbacks of the past decade, Don Meredith and Craig Morton, has all of those qualities. From 1971 until Morton was traded to the New York Giants, Staubach and Morton battled in the preseason for the starting job but no matter how well Morton did, Roger always got the job. The only time after 1971 that he surrendered it was because of injury.

Staubach also determined much of his own success from the moment he signed a Cowboys' contract, before his career as a naval officer hardly had begun. He spent a year in Vietnam and took along an NFL football. He spent two weeks of his leave one summer at the Cowboys' training camp. He became the first player ever allowed to take home a Cowboys' playbook in the off-season. And he studied

In 1971, Roger Staubach told coach Landry, "Play me or trade me." By midseason he was number one quarterback.

miles of Dallas game film when others were out at the PX movie.

Staubach was a future draft choice of both the Cowboys and Kansas City in 1964. Dallas signed him to a $10,000 a year contract soon after his graduation from Annapolis, the only stipulation being that he would join the Cowboys if and when his navy career ended.

Thanks to his extracurricular football work, and three seasons of service football, his skills never rusted. If there was a problem it was where he could fit in with the Cowboys because Meredith and Morton still were there when he went to his first training camp. Staubach expected to wind up with another team, but Meredith retired just days before camp began.

All Roger needed was preparation and experience—the Landry way. It was not necessarily the Staubach way, though his coach predicted at the time he would be a starter in the NFL within three seasons.

"When I first came to the team," Staubach admits, "I fought the system. Tom had told me it takes three to five years for a quarterback to mature in pro football. I didn't believe him. I was in tremendous mental and physical shape. More than that, I had the confidence that if I were given the opportunity to play, I could win."

Morton was injured in the preseason and Staubach started the first game of the 1969 season against St. Louis. Dallas won 24-3 but there were a few memorable moments, including his seven completions for 220 yards, one a 75-yard scoring pass, and his first NFL touchdown.

That day he was vintage Roger the Dodger. On one play he scrambled for nearly half a minute and was so winded he could hardly call the next play. Scrambling quarterbacks are not Landry's bag but he realized that Staubach did it because he wasn't yet prepared to cope with the NFL.

Some teams, such as Detroit with Greg Landry, run their quarterback several times during a game. Not Tom Landry, even with Staubach's known ability.

"Funny thing," 49ers defensive end Cedrick Hardman says, "but Staubach is a niftier runner than Greg Landry."

In a crucial game against Washington a few years ago, Staubach ran 29 yards for the winning touchdown but it didn't move Landry to change.

"He does what he must do," Landry said, shrugging, "and he does it well. We'll have no plays where Roger is supposed to run. He runs enough without plays."

Nor can he be compared to Fran Tarkenton, the "original" scrambler. The difference, according to Cowboys president Tex Schramm, is that Staubach is a better passer and just as effective a runner.

For the rest of 1969, Staubach did not play much as Dallas won its fourth title in a row but lost to Cleveland in the Eastern Conference playoffs. In 1970, the Cow-

boys made it to the Super Bowl, losing in the last five seconds to Baltimore. Morton had a bad arm that year and barely was able to throw. Staubach started the season at quarterback, got two victories, then lost to the Cardinals. He was sent back to the bench and saw little action after that.

The bench-sitting bothered him. Before the start of training camp in 1971, he went to Landry.

"I had to get on with it," he recalls. "My prospects didn't look good sitting on the bench. I knew I could play. All I wanted was a chance. I wanted to be a starter, to have a full career, if not in Dallas then someplace else.

"I told Landry and said if he did not have confidence in me for the coming season, the best thing to do was trade me."

Landry did a bit of everything at the start of that season. He started Staubach. He started Morton—he alternated them on every play. And the Cowboys spun their wheels. At midseason they were 4-3 and Landry finally made his move. Roger was to be number one quarterback.

Dallas did not lose another game, including a 24-3 drubbing of Miami in the Super Bowl. In winning the most valuable player award for that game, Staubach threw two touchdown passes, completed 12 of 19 for 100 yards, and even scrambled a bit.

He had just about come of age. Landry was calling all the plays but Staubach, with just four interceptions, won the NFL passing title.

In 1972, Landry again pitted Morton against Staubach in the preseason for the starting job. But that competition ended quickly when Roger tried to run over Rams linebacker Marlin McKeever for a touchdown and suffered a dislocated shoulder. It wasn't until the last quarter of the first playoff game against San Francisco that he became a factor.

The 49ers seemingly had that game wrapped up, leading 28-13 in the fourth quarter, when Landry changed quarterbacks. In came Staubach. He did little until the final two minutes. Then he fired two touchdown passes and helped give the Cowboys a stunning 30-28 victory.

Roger is a young quarterback in terms of NFL experience. He has a strong arm and tremendous leadership ability.

Landry was convinced Staubach should start the next week against Washington for the NFC title, though Morton had been the number one quarterback all season. It didn't work out. There was too much rust on Staubach's skills and the Redskins won the title.

The next season, Staubach was number one again—with the Cowboys and as an NFL passer. Dallas won the NFC East title in the fourth quarter of its playoff game against Los Angeles. Dallas led only 17-16 with the ball at its 17-yard line. It was

third-and-14 against a team that had taken control of the game.

Landry sent in a pass play to Bob Hayes but Staubach altered wide receiver Drew Pearson to run a slant pattern. He rifled the ball to Pearson, who caught it between two defenders and ran for the clinching touchdown.

Still a young quarterback in terms of experience, many feel Staubach's best years at the NFL still lay ahead. He agrees, remembering some parental advice he received back in Purcell High School in

Coach Landry says, "We have no plays on which Roger is supposed to run. He runs well enough without plays."

Cincinnati.

"Being a hero seemed like a big deal then," he says. "But my parents kept telling me I was just on one plateau, that if I thought I was so great on that plateau, I wasn't going to achieve another level."

That's Staubach the football player. There is much more to him than football. One of his best qualities is his concern about what effect his image will have on young people. He has been called "square" because he rejects many of the current trends but that doesn't bother him.

He is an active member in the Fellowship of Christian Athletes but never touts his faith or beliefs. Yet he does not hesitate to express them if asked.

He has bypassed important commercial endorsements because he didn't like the image they portrayed. Still, he does not condemn those who are considered "swingers," saying simply that that kind of life "isn't my style."

He doesn't forcibly try to change any minds to his way of thinking—except, perhaps, Tom Landry's.

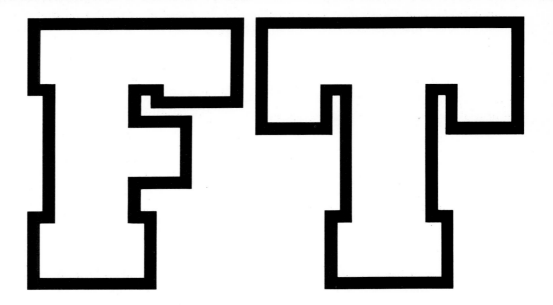

Fran Tarkenton   Minnesota Vikings

Fran Tarkenton has played quarterback in the National Football League since 1961 and when he finally does retire, he could hold every major passing record—ahead of such players as Johnny Unitas, Y. A. Tittle, and Sonny Jurgensen.

No matter what achievements finally may be his, Tarkenton always will be remembered for one thing—scrambling. Trace his career from its beginning with the Minnesota Vikings, through his time with the New York Giants and back again to the Vikings and there still is one over-riding theme. He is "The Scrambler."

He doesn't scramble much any more, certainly not the way he once did. There were times when he would run around for incredible periods of time while defensive linemen chased, grabbed, and lunged in maddening futility. There he would be, dodging and darting, running forward, then backward, then back even farther—so far sometimes that if he completed a pass, it would be considered "long" though it might wind up just a four-yard gain.

While he scrambled, it became a rule of thumb for his offensive line to stay put. "He'll be coming back this way in a bit," they'd say. "There'll be someone to block."

Often, some said, you'd hear a familiar cry: "Look out, here he comes again!"

And the blockers would try to clear a path.

Downfield, another scene would be played. When Tarkenton scrambled, all his receivers would stop whatever pattern they were running and go in the same direction as their quarterback. When he changed direction, they'd do the same.

But there is more to Fran Tarkenton than being just a scrambling quarterback, trying to make something out of a busted play. He has executed many plays that weren't busted, plays that were big in every sense of the word. He's gained more than 35,000 yards passing. Only Unitas, with 40,239, has gained more. And only Unitas stands ahead of him in number of touchdown passes and completions.

All that running—more than 3,500 yards—has made him the all-time rusher among pro quarterbacks. No one else is even close.

Those figures represent some milestones in Tarkenton's career. He's gone through quite a bit to achieve them. He was the first starting quarterback the Vikings ever had; a hero during five years in New York with the Giants; a losing quarterback in two Super Bowls; a man who battled his first pro coach in public print so that both were forced to leave; and perhaps the most durable quarterback in terms of service ever.

Two men with sideline 'cool': Fran Tarkenton discusses game strategy with coach Bud Grant.

Everyone calls him Francis. His father is a minister. But Francis has had his share of scraps and tossed a few salty phrases. With the Giants, he once threw a football at the Redskins' defensive end after being roughed up. That started a mini-brawl. In a couple of games against the Jets, he did the same thing, one of them igniting his scrambling style. He hasn't always appreciated the reputation but accepts it.

"When I first joined the Vikings," he says, "everybody would see me scramble and they'd say, 'He'll get killed doing that!' But it turned out that staying in the pocket in those days was no guarantee of safety. Sure, I took my lumps, but in my first six seasons with the Vikings, I missed only two quarters because of injury."

Being a "scrambler," he maintains, is all a matter of semantics.

Barely six feet tall, Fran has to throw quickly to get his passes by people such as the Rams' Jack Reynolds.

Fran was with the New York Giants from 1967 through 1971. Here he is on a typical scrambling play against Dallas.

"I usually know where I'm going to throw when I take the snap," says Fran. "Certainly by the second step backward."

"I throw from the pocket, I use play-action, I sprint out. What gets me is to see a quarterback give up because his protection breaks down and he doesn't try to make something out of the play."

When he first came to the Giants in 1967, he joined a team that had sagged badly since the championship years of the early 1960s. Tarkenton struck lightning and thunder in Yankee Stadium with his epic passes to wide receiver Homer Jones.

At that time, Jones ranked with the Cowboys' Bob Hayes in the NFL for the combination of speed and pass-catching ability. As Francis did his scrambling routine, Jones became deadly effective. The longer Tarkenton could elude tacklers, the more

time Jones had to break into the clear. Though not known as a "bomb thrower," Tarkenton became just that because Jones caught 13 touchdown passes and averaged a whopping 25 yards on each of his 49 receptions the first season the two played together.

The best current assessment of Tarkenton is made by Minnesota coach Bud Grant who was the force behind the Vikings' reacquisition of Francis from the Giants after the 1971 season. Grant is a bread-and-butter coach who believes games are won by execution.

"Fran is very confident, he's very intelligent, and he's very observant," Grant says. "He selects plays well and he builds a drive soundly. He doesn't waste plays. He explores a defense well. He is one of the best at going to the open man on a pass pattern. When no one's open, he's wise enough to throw the ball away and not force the pass. He plays the percentages."

Tarkenton's own football philosophy is similar and dilutes the common impression that he makes things up as he goes along. Oh, he's been known to step into a huddle and call something that's not in the game plan, something that he just remembered using two or three games before. But basically, he's a block-builder.

"To me, a five-minute, eighty-yard drive in which you inch out yards and pick away at chinks in the defense with short passes is more interesting than a one-shot, eighty-yard touchdown pass," Tarkenton says. "You must outguess and outmaneuver the defense and still avoid mistakes like penalties, fumbles, and interceptions that can spoil your work."

On the field, he makes sure it is his work. A former Giants' wide receiver who had played with Y. A. Tittle in New York once complained, "With Y. A. you could come back and tell him a certain pass was open and he'd go to it. Francis looked at you like he never heard you and I don't really think he wanted to."

"The way defenses now change with every play, I make up my own mind," Tarkenton says. "What might look open to a receiver on one play might never be there again. I usually know where I'm going to throw when I take the snap, certainly by my second step backward. That's experience—knowing the defense and its tendencies, knowing personnel."

That philosophy is tailored to his own physical limitations. He does not have a great arm and the one he has has given him problems since he returned to the Vikings. Francis says he can throw a football 62½ yards because he measured the distance.

"If I wait for an end to run out sixty-one-and-a-half yards, it's too late," he says. "But distance just doesn't mean that much."

Though barely 6 feet and less than 200 pounds, he has been amazingly injury-free during his pro career. And he has taken plenty of shots running, maybe with extra relish by defensive linemen who have found his maddening scrambles a cruel form of torture.

He came off the bench in the first regular season game the Vikings ever played—an astounding upset of the Chicago Bears—and did not miss a game until 1971 when Alex Webster, then coach of the Giants, benched him in the final game of the season. Webster admitted later that he did not know Tarkenton had a streak of 153 consecutive games or he would have allowed it to continue.

Part of Tarkenton's injury-free secret is that he knows where the trouble is and how to avoid it. If he's in trouble, he doesn't anticipate being tackled—he goes down himself before impact; or he runs out of bounds before a defensive back can get him. Of course, being with a championship team helps, too.

Francis always has given the impression that he knows where he's going and how he's going to get there—on and off the field. In 1966, when he and Vikings coach Norm Van Brocklin got into violent disputes during his first tour with the Vikings, Tarkenton wrote to the team management and said he no longer wanted to play for Minnesota.

The situation deteriorated, and Van Brocklin resigned and Tarkenton was traded to the Giants. Van Brocklin then fired off his long-remembered appraisal of his former quarterback.

"He'll win games he's not supposed to win and he'll lose games he's not supposed to lose but he'll never win a big game," the volatile Dutchman said.

That statement is open to challenge. Tarkenton has helped the Vikings win a couple of NFC title games but he still hasn't quarterbacked a Super Bowl champion. But then neither have a lot of eminent quarterbacks. And after the team's loss to Miami in Super Bowl VIII Tarkenton donated his entire loser's check of $7,500 to funds for ailing and handicapped children.

That might help win a bigger game than Van Brocklin had in mind.

How to Play Quarterback

Ball-Handling: Taking the Snap

Taking the snap properly is very important. The center brings the football up to your passing hand and your free hand guides it in. Good teamwork here prevents fumbles.

About to Hand Off

Holding the ball with both hands, step toward the runner with the onside foot. Move out fast so you can make the handoff on time and make it right.

About to Pass

The proper ball-handling when you are about to pass is to turn the football in your hands so your fingers are across the laces. This gives you good control.

Footwork

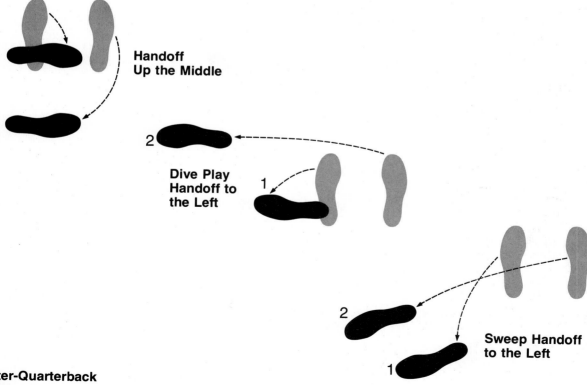

Handoff Up the Middle

Dive Play Handoff to the Left

Sweep Handoff to the Left

The Center-Quarterback Exchange

The Handoff

When handing off, remember that running backs may have different likes and dislikes for the way they take the football. Some may like a scoop, as shown in the upper photo, and some may like to take the ball in the overhand style. As quarterback, you have to keep this in mind and make the handoff accordingly. "Look" the ball into the target—the runner's bread basket. Then keep moving and don't give the play away by stopping dead still to watch the runner.

The Pitch

To get the ball to a running
back, you can either hand
it off to him, or pitch
it to him. This can be
very effective, especially
when a fast-moving back
takes a quick toss and
scoots around his own end
before the defense can react.
For this kind of a pitch,
take the ball just as you
get it from the center and
flip it to the runner
with both hands.
On a pitch play that takes
longer to develop, you
have time to turn and
make a more careful toss.

arterbacks have to be good
sers. If you are going to
ome one, you must learn
eliver the ball with a
ooth passing motion. First,
it slightly back of its
ter with your fingers
ead and on the laces.

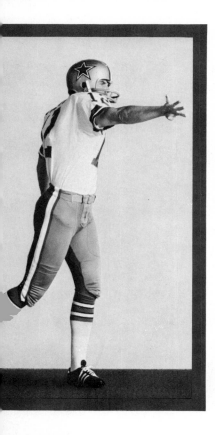

g the ball forward in an
rhead motion. Don't throw
dearm. Snap your wrist
turn your hand over as you
w through, to give the ball
al. Throw the ball smoothly
relaxed manner; never
e it.

Getting to the Pocket

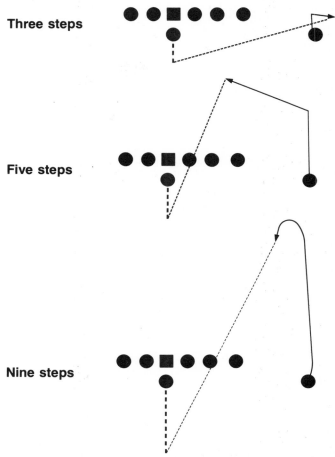

Three steps

Five steps

Nine steps

Some passes develop more quickly than others, and
as quarterback you have to know the appropriate
number of steps for each of them. For a quick out,
take three steps back and hit your receiver with the
pass quickly. For a turn-in route, five steps are
needed. The nine-step drop is correct for a slow-
developing deep pass such as a curl pattern.

Back-Pedaling

Turning to Drop Back

Play-Action Passes

Fake a Run...

... and Pass

A play-action pass is one that starts out looking as if it's going to be a run but ends up being a pass. It often can fool the defense into coming up to stop the run and being out of position on the pass. As quarterback, you fake a handoff, then find the open receiver and throw. The more convincing the handoff fake, the more offguard the defense is going to be. So you have a good chance for a completion

Rolling Out

You won't always be passing from the pocket. Occasionally you'll be rolling out, too. It is easier to roll out to the side of your passing arm than it is to roll out the other way. Lead your receiver—throw the ball a few yards ahead of him and let him catch up to it —when rolling out to your passing arm side. Don't lead him when going the other way; the natural curve in the throw is missing when you roll out "against the grain". In each case, turn your body around to square up with the target before you pass.

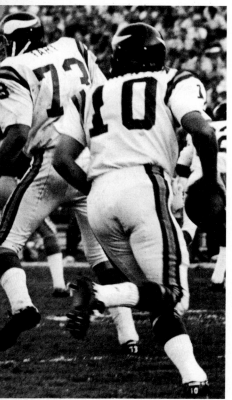

Lead your receiver on your throwing arm side

Don't when going the other way

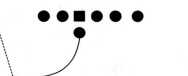

95

Finding Your Receivers

One of the hardest things you will ever have to learn as a quarterback will be to find your receivers. First, you will have to locate a little bit of daylight through the rushing defensive linemen to get your pass through them. At the same time, looking downfield, you must sight an opening through the linebackers' zones. And you have only a few seconds to do all this. Once you can, you'll be a real quarterback!

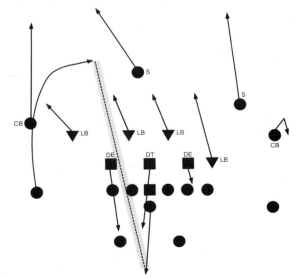